Oxford English Picture Dictionary

牛津英漢圖畫字典

E C PARNWELL

Illustrations by
Corinne Clarke and Ray Burrows

梁璐如譯

OXFORD
IN ASIA

牛津大學出版社

Oxford University Press

文鶴出版有限公司

怎樣用這本字典

要找尋某一件物品的英文名稱，先要查目錄，找出那一頁插圖可能會有你所需要的字。每一件物品，都分門別類地歸納在一起，例如：所有動物的英文名稱，都會列在「動物」和「在農場」的插圖頁裏。當你翻到所需要的插圖頁時，你會看到圖中所有的動物都編有號碼。在圖的下方，憑着編號，你便可以找出你所要找的動物的英文名稱。找到你需要的字後，可以試試學習一些在同一頁的其他有關生字，然後把生字蓋起來，看看能記得多少。

由八十二頁起是本字典的索引。在索引裏，你會找到書中所收的英文字依着字母次序全部排列出來。每個字的後面都附有音標符號，幫助你怎樣讀出這些生字。此外，字後還有兩個號碼，例如26 / 3，第一個號碼告訴你要找的物品的頁數，第二個號碼告訴你生字所指的物件的圖樣。

Oxford University Press

OXFORD LONDON GLASGOW

NEW YORK TORONTO MELBOURNE AUCKLAND

KUALA LUMPUR SINGAPORE HONG KONG TOKYO

DELHI BOMBAY CALCUTTA MADRAS KARACHI

NAIROBI DAR ES SALAAM CAPE TOWN SALISBURY

and associates in

BEIRUT BERLIN IBADAN MEXICO CITY NICOSIA

© *Oxford University Press 1979*

First published 1979

This edition reprinted with permission by the Crane Publishing Co.
Ltd. and is only for sale within Taiwan

©牛津大學出版社1979

1979年初版

此版本由牛津大學出版社批准

文鶴出版有限公司出版

祇可在台灣境內出售

ISBN 0 19 581203 4

OXFORD is a trademark of Oxford University Press.

CONTENTS 目錄

In Space A.	在太空	new/crescent moon 11	新月／上弦月
comet 1	彗星	half moon 12	半月
constellation 2	星座	full moon 13	滿月
galaxy 3	星系，銀河系	old moon 14	缺月／下弦月
planet 4	行星		
star 5	星	Space-travel C.	太空飛行
Moon 6	月亮	nosecone 15	火箭頭
Earth 7	地球	rocket 16	火箭
Sun 8	太陽	launching-pad 17	發射台
orbit 9	運行軌道	satellite 18	人造衛星
		(space-)capsule 19	（太空）密閉小艙
Phases of the Moon B.	月相	astronaut 20	太空飛行員
eclipse 10	月蝕	spacesuit 21	太空衣

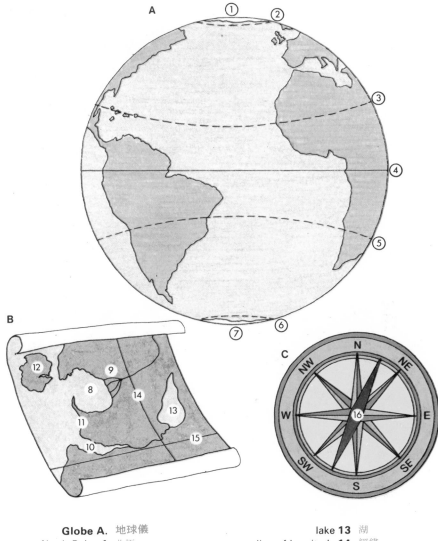

Globe A.		地球儀	lake	**13** 湖
North Pole	**1**	北極	line of longitude	**14** 經綫
Arctic Circle	**2**	北極圈	line of latitude	**15** 緯綫
Tropic of Cancer	**3**	北回歸綫		
Equator	**4**	赤道	**Compass C.**	羅盤
Tropic of Capricorn	**5**	南回歸綫	needle	**16** 羅盤指針
Antarctic Circle	**6**	南極圈	N	north 北
South Pole	**7**	南極	NE	northeast 東北
			E	east 東
Map B.		地圖	SE	southeast 東南
bay	**8**	海灣	S	south 南
delta	**9**	三角洲	SW	southwest 西南
estuary	**10**	河口灣	W	west 西
coastline	**11**	海岸綫	NW	northwest 西北
island	**12**	海島		

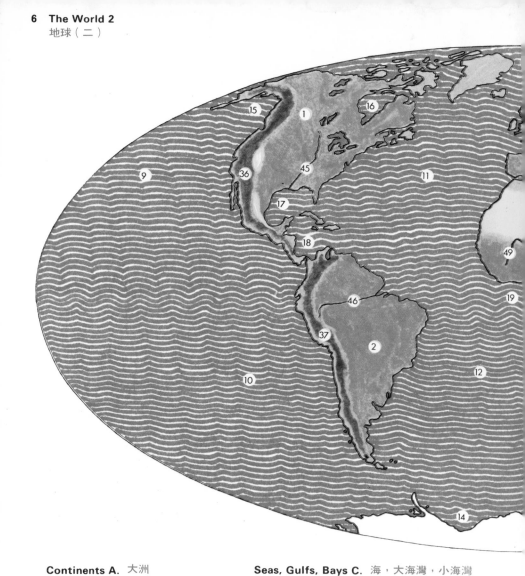

Continents A. 大洲		
North America	**1**	北美洲
South America	**2**	南美洲
Europe	**3**	歐洲
Africa	**4**	非洲
Asia	**5**	亞洲
Australia	**6**	澳洲
Antarctica	**7**	南極洲

Oceans B. 大洋		
Arctic	**8**	北冰洋
North Pacific	**9**	北太平洋
South Pacific	**10**	南太平洋
North Atlantic	**11**	北大西洋
South Atlantic	**12**	南大西洋
Indian	**13**	印度洋
South	**14**	南冰洋

Seas, Gulfs, Bays C. 海，大海灣，小海灣		
Gulf of Alaska	**15**	阿拉斯加灣
Hudson Bay	**16**	赫德遜灣
Gulf of Mexico	**17**	墨西哥灣
Caribbean Sea	**18**	加勒比海
Gulf of Guinea	**19**	畿內亞灣
North Sea	**20**	北海
Baltic Sea	**21**	波羅的海
Mediterranean Sea	**22**	地中海
Black Sea	**23**	黑海
Caspian Sea	**24**	裏海
Red Sea	**25**	紅海
Persian Gulf	**26**	波斯灣
Arabian Sea	**27**	阿拉伯海
Bay of Bengal	**28**	孟加拉灣
Coral Sea	**29**	珊瑚海
Tasman Sea	**30**	塔斯馬海

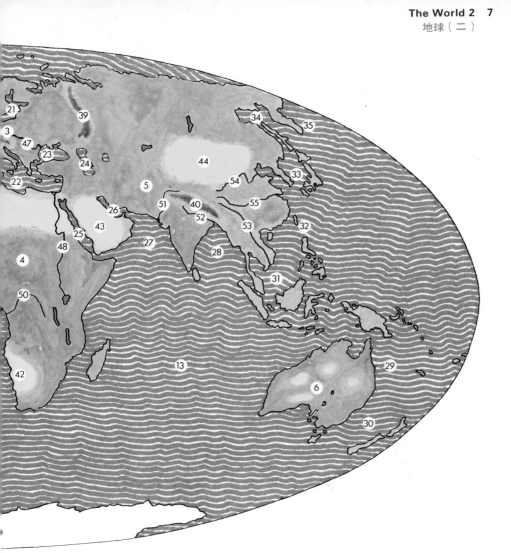

South China Sea **31**	南中國海	**Rivers F.**	河流
East China Sea **32**	東中國海	Mississippi **45**	密西西比河
Sea of Japan **33**	日本海	Amazon **46**	亞馬遜河
Sea of Okhotsk **34**	鄂霍次克海	Danube **47**	多瑙河
Bering Sea **35**	白令海	Nile **48**	尼羅河
		Niger **49**	尼日爾河
Mountain ranges D.	山脈	Congo **50**	剛果河
Rockies **36**	落磯山脈	Indus **51**	印度河
Andes **37**	安第斯山脈	Ganges **52**	恆河
Alps **38**	阿爾卑斯山脈	Mekong **53**	湄公河
Urals **39**	烏拉山脈	Hwang (Yellow) **54**	黃河
Himalayas **40**	喜馬拉雅山脈	Yangtze **55**	長江‧揚子江
Deserts E.	沙漠		
Sahara **41**	撒哈拉沙漠		
Kalahari **42**	喀拉哈利沙漠		
Arabian **43**	阿拉伯沙漠		
Gobi **44**	戈壁沙漠		

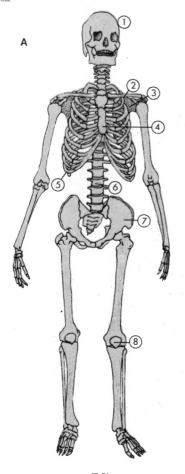

A

B

The skeleton A. 骨骼

skull	**1**	頭蓋骨
collar-bone	**2**	鎖骨
shoulder-blade	**3**	肩胛骨
breastbone	**4**	胸骨
rib	**5**	肋骨
backbone/spine	**6**	脊骨
hip-bone/pelvis	**7**	盆骨
kneecap	**8**	膝蓋

The body B. 身體

hair	**9**	頭髮
head	**10**	頭
neck	**11**	頸
throat	**12**	咽喉
shoulder	**13**	肩膀
chest	**14**	胸
back	**15**	背
waist	**16**	腰
stomach/tummy	**17**	腹

hip	**18**	股
bottom/buttocks	**19**	臀部
armpit	**20**	腋下
arm	**21**	手臂
upper arm	**22**	上臂
elbow	**23**	肘
forearm	**24**	前臂
wrist	**25**	手腕
fist	**26**	拳（頭）
hand	**27**	手
palm	**28**	手掌
thumb	**29**	大拇指
finger	**30**	手指
nail	**31**	指甲
leg	**32**	腿
thigh	**33**	大腿
knee	**34**	膝
calf	**35**	小腿
ankle	**36**	足踝
foot	**37**	脚

人體

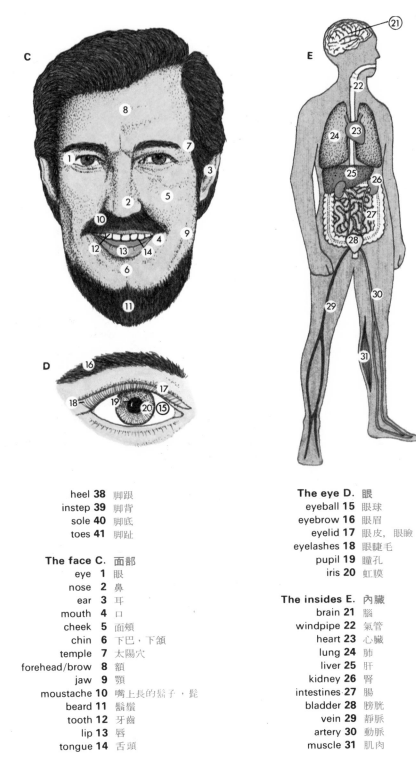

heel **38** 脚跟
instep **39** 脚背
sole **40** 脚底
toes **41** 脚趾

The face C. 面部
eye **1** 眼
nose **2** 鼻
ear **3** 耳
mouth **4** 口
cheek **5** 面頰
chin **6** 下巴，下頷
temple **7** 太陽穴
forehead/brow **8** 額
jaw **9** 顎
moustache **10** 嘴上長的鬍子，髭
beard **11** 鬍鬚
tooth **12** 牙齒
lip **13** 唇
tongue **14** 舌頭

The eye D. 眼
eyeball **15** 眼球
eyebrow **16** 眼眉
eyelid **17** 眼皮，眼瞼
eyelashes **18** 眼睫毛
pupil **19** 瞳孔
iris **20** 虹膜

The insides E. 內臟
brain **21** 腦
windpipe **22** 氣管
heart **23** 心臟
lung **24** 肺
liver **25** 肝
kidney **26** 腎
intestines **27** 腸
bladder **28** 膀胱
vein **29** 靜脈
artery **30** 動脈
muscle **31** 肌肉

vest	**1**	汗衫	wellington(-boot) **10**	威靈頓長靴
pants	**2**	內褲	T-shirt **11**	圓領緊身男汗衫
dressing-gown	**3**	晨衣，晨褸	shorts **12**	短褲
pyjamas	**4**	睡衣	cardigan **13**	開襟絨綫衫
slipper	**5**	拖鞋	sock **14**	襪
jumper	**6**	套頭毛衣	plimsoll/gym-shoe/ **15**	運動鞋
jeans	**7**	牛仔褲	tennis-shoe	
jacket	**8**	外衣	cap **16**	軟帽
shoe	**9**	鞋		

shirt	**1**	襯衣，恤衫	
collar	**2**	領	
cuff	**3**	袖口	
tie	**4**	領帶	
waistcoat	**5**	背心	
suit	**6**	一套西服	
sleeve	**7**	袖	
shoe	**8**	鞋	
shoelace	**9**	鞋帶	
sole	**10**	鞋底	
heel	**11**	鞋跟	
raincoat/mackintosh/	**12**	雨衣	
mac			

hat	**13**	帽
coat	**14**	大衣
lapel	**15**	翻領
pocket	**16**	口袋，袋
trousers	**17**	長褲
turn-up	**18**	摺邊
scarf	**19**	領巾
glove	**20**	手套
watch	**21**	手錶
watch-strap	**22**	錶帶
glasses	**23**	眼鏡
umbrella	**24**	雨傘

bra/brassière	**1**	乳罩	
slip/petticoat	**2**	底裙	
pants	**3**	內褲	
tights	**4**	緊身長褲	
shawl	**5**	披肩	
nightdress/	**6**	睡袍	
nightgown			
slipper	**7**	拖鞋	
ring	**8**	指環，戒指	
bracelet	**9**	手鐲	
ear-ring	**10**	耳環	

necklace	**11**	項鍊	
nail-file	**12**	指甲銼	
(powder-)compact	**13**	粉盒	
mascara	**14**	染睫毛（或眉毛）油	
nail-varnish/-polish	**15**	指甲油	
scent/perfume	**16**	香水	
eye shadow	**17**	眼蓋膏	
face-cream	**18**	面霜	
lipstick	**19**	唇膏，口紅	

blouse	**1**	罩衫		coat	**9**	大衣
skirt	**2**	裙		belt	**10**	衣帶
sock	**3**	襪		buckle	**11**	扣
hat	**4**	帽		shoe	**12**	鞋
jersey/jumper/	**5**	短上衣，套衫		scarf	**13**	領巾
sweater/pullover				handkerchief	**14**	手帕
trousers	**6**	長褲		brooch	**15**	別針，胸針
sandal	**7**	涼鞋		(hand)bag	**16**	（手）袋
dress	**8**	衣連裙		umbrella	**17**	雨傘

letter-box	**1**	郵筒	gutter	**10**	明溝
(pedestrian) crossing	**2**	（行人）橫過處	drain	**11**	暗溝
stall (in the market)	**3**	（街市）貨攤	park	**12**	公園
barrow	**4**	手推車	bridge	**13**	橋
taxi	**5**	計程車，的士	van	**14**	小型貨車
bicycle	**6**	腳踏車，自行車	lorry	**15**	貨車
traffic-light	**7**	交通燈	crossroads	**16**	十字路口
signpost	**8**	路標	motorbike/cycle	**17**	摩托車，電單車
kerb	**9**	路緣石	pram	**18**	嬰兒車

(block of) flats **19** （一幢）大廈	bus-stop **28** 公共汽車停車處
office-block **20** 辦公室大廈	pavement **29** 行人路
advertisement **21** 廣告	litter-bin/-basket **30** 廢物箱／簍
shop **22** 商店	(tele)phone-box/ **31** 電話亭
shop-window **23** 窗櫥	call-box
lamp-post **24** 燈柱	car-park **32** 停車場
parking-meter **25** 停車收費錶	car **33** 汽車
bus **26** 公共汽車，巴士	road/street **34** 路／街
(bus-)conductor **27** （公共汽車）售票員	

Detection A.		偵查
policeman	**1**	警察
helmet	**2**	頭盔
uniform	**3**	制服
police-station	**4**	警署，警察局
police-car	**5**	警車
police-dog	**6**	警犬
truncheon	**7**	警棍
handcuffs	**8**	手銬
torch	**9**	手電筒
magnifying-glass	**10**	放大鏡
fingerprints	**11**	指模，指紋
footprints	**12**	脚印

Prison/Jail/Gaol B.		監獄
warder	**13**	監獄看守
prisoner	**14**	囚犯
cell	**15**	牢房，囚室
bars	**16**	柵

Law court C.		法庭
jury	**17**	陪審團，陪審員
witness-box	**18**	證人席
witness	**19**	證人
defendant/accused	**20**	被告
dock	**21**	被告席
judge	**22**	法官
lawyer	**23**	律師
gown/robe	**24**	長袍
wig	**25**	假髮

Fire brigade/	**A.**	消防隊／消防事務
Fire service		
fireman	**1**	消防員
helmet	**2**	頭盔
hose(pipe)	**3**	水喉管
nozzle	**4**	噴嘴
hydrant	**5**	消防栓
(fire-)extinguisher	**6**	滅火器
fire-engine	**7**	救火車
ladder	**8**	雲梯
bell	**9**	鈴
fire-escape	**10**	走火通道，太平梯
fire	**11**	火
smoke	**12**	烟
flame	**13**	火焰
At the dentist	**B.**	在牙醫診所
dental nurse	**14**	牙醫護士
dentist's chair	**15**	牙科椅子

dentist	**16**	牙醫
drill	**17**	牙鑽
light	**18**	燈
A hospital ward	**C.**	醫院病房
(hospital) bed	**19**	病床
patient	**20**	病人
doctor	**21**	醫生
stethoscope	**22**	聽診器，聽筒
sling	**23**	吊帶
X-ray	**24**	X光
nurse	**25**	護士
crutch	**26**	拐杖
bandage	**27**	繃帶
thermometer	**28**	溫度計，體溫計，探熱針
(box of) pills	**29**	（一盒）藥丸
(bottle of) medicine	**30**	（一瓶）藥水
(medicine) spoon	**31**	藥匙
stretcher	**32**	擔架

teacher	**1**	教師，老師	pencil	**15**	鉛筆
blackboard	**2**	黑板	set-square	**16**	三角板，三角尺
easel	**3**	黑板架	pen	**17**	筆
chalk	**4**	粉筆	exercise-book	**18**	練習簿
duster	**5**	粉刷	textbook	**19**	課本
platform	**6**	講台，教壇	slide-rule	**20**	計算尺
desk	**7**	書桌	map	**21**	地圖
schoolgirl/pupil	**8**	女學生／學生	timetable	**22**	時間表
satchel/schoolbag	**9**	書包	calendar	**23**	日曆
ruler	**10**	尺	poster	**24**	海報
compasses	**11**	圓規	paintbrushes	**25**	畫筆
protractor	**12**	量角器	palette	**26**	調色板
glue/gum	**13**	膠水	paints	**27**	顏料
rubber	**14**	像皮，擦紙膠			

balance/scales	1	天秤	Bunsen burner	12	本生燈
pan	2	秤盤	tripod	13	三脚架
weights	3	砝碼	rubber tubing	14	橡皮管
meter	4	量錶	beaker	15	燒杯
dial	5	刻度盤	flask	16	燒瓶
needle/pointer	6	指針	crystals	17	晶體
bench	7	工作枱	pipette	18	吸量管
stool	8	櫈子	magnet	19	磁鐵，磁石
microscope	9	顯微鏡	pestle	20	杵
lens	10	鏡片	mortar	21	臼
slide	11	承物玻璃片	test-tube	22	試管

shop-window	**1**	櫥窗	
cashier	**2**	出納員	
cash-register	**3**	收銀機	
cash-desk	**4**	收款處	
customer	**5**	顧客	
(carrier-)bag	**6**	（手提）袋	
basket	**7**	籃子	
(shop-)assistant	**8**	店員	
cheese	**9**	乳酪，芝士	
milk	**10**	牛奶	
eggs	**11**	蛋	
sausages	**12**	香腸	
meat	**13**	肉	

deep-freeze/freezer	**14**	冷藏櫃
shelf	**15**	擱板
tinned food	**16**	罐頭食品
fruit	**17**	水果
vegetables	**18**	蔬菜
bread	**19**	麵飽
biscuits	**20**	餅乾
cakes	**21**	蛋糕
counter	**22**	櫃台
receipt	**23**	收據
(bank-)notes	**24**	紙幣
coins	**25**	輔幣，硬幣

desk	**1**	辦公桌		letter basket	**12**	信簍
telephone	**2**	電話		wastepaper-basket	**13**	廢紙簍
adding-machine/	**3**	加數機／計算機		fan	**14**	風扇
calculator				switchboard	**15**	電話接綫台
blotter/blotting-pad	**4**	吸墨水紙		operator	**16**	電話接綫生
diary	**5**	日記簿		calendar	**17**	日曆
(hole-)punch	**6**	打孔機		file	**18**	文件夾
stapler	**7**	釘書機		filing-cabinet	**19**	文件櫃
staple	**8**	釘書釘		carbon-paper	**20**	複寫紙
paper-clip	**9**	紙夾		typewriter	**21**	打字機
(sheet of) paper	**10**	（一張）紙		secretary/typist	**22**	秘書／打字員
envelope	**11**	信封		notebook/notepad	**23**	記事簿

clerk	**1**	郵務員	writing-paper	**12**	信紙
scales	**2**	磅	postcard	**13**	明信片
counter	**3**	櫃台	envelope	**14**	信封
letter-box/post-box/	**4**	郵筒	flap	**15**	摺口，封口
pillar-box			telegram/cable	**16**	電報
postman	**5**	郵差	postal order	**17**	郵政滙票
mailbag	**6**	郵袋	seal	**18**	印章
airletter	**7**	航空郵箋，航空郵簡	sealing-wax	**19**	火漆
postmark	**8**	郵戳	parcel	**20**	包裹
stamp	**9**	郵票	string	**21**	繩
(airmail-)letter	**10**	（航空）信	label	**22**	標籤
address	**11**	地址			

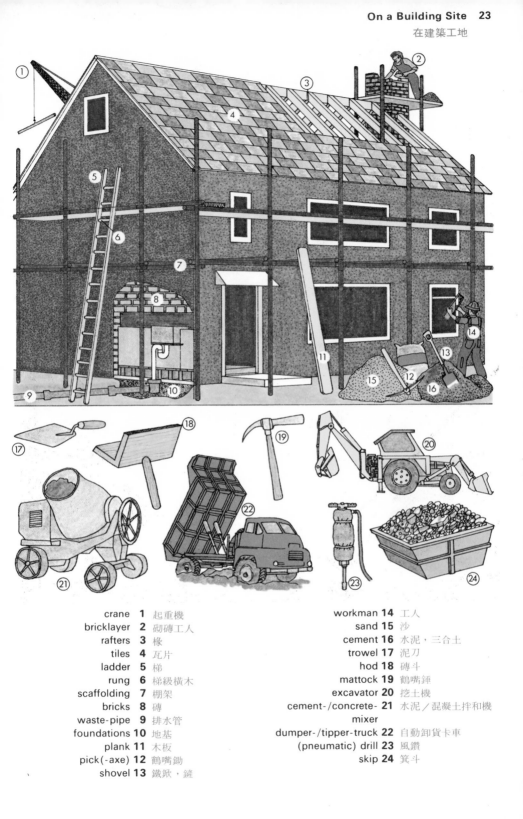

crane	**1**	起重機	workman **14**	工人
bricklayer	**2**	砌磚工人	sand **15**	沙
rafters	**3**	椽	cement **16**	水泥，三合土
tiles	**4**	瓦片	trowel **17**	泥刀
ladder	**5**	梯	hod **18**	磚斗
rung	**6**	梯級橫木	mattock **19**	鶴嘴錘
scaffolding	**7**	棚架	excavator **20**	挖土機
bricks	**8**	磚	cement-/concrete- **21**	水泥／混凝土拌和機
waste-pipe	**9**	排水管	mixer	
foundations	**10**	地基	dumper-/tipper-truck **22**	自動卸貨卡車
plank	**11**	木板	(pneumatic) drill **23**	風鑽
pick(-axe)	**12**	鶴嘴鋤	skip **24**	箕斗
shovel	**13**	鐵鍁，鏟		

(work)bench	**1**	工作枱	spade	**9**	鏟
file	**2**	銼	(garden) fork	**10**	草叉
sandpaper	**3**	沙紙	shears	**11**	大剪刀
chisel	**4**	鑿子	trowel	**12**	小鏟子
(pen-)knife	**5**	小刀	spanner	**13**	扳手
wrench	**6**	扳鉗	pincers	**14**	胡桃鉗
screwdriver	**7**	螺絲起子	chopper	**15**	砍刀
vice	**8**	老虎鉗			

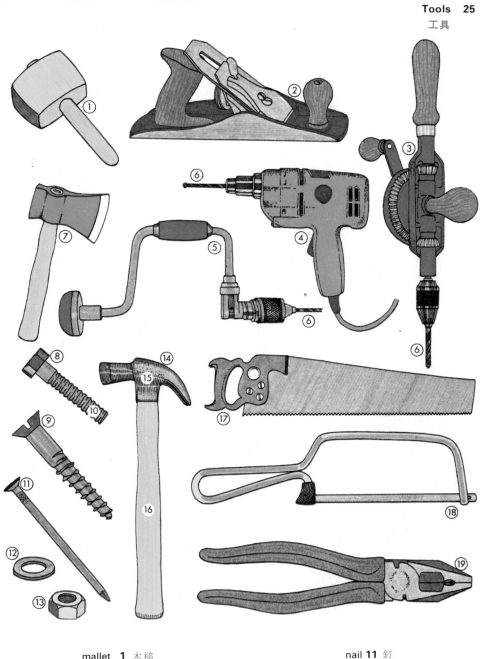

mallet **1** 木槌
plane **2** 刨
hand-drill **3** 手鑽
electric drill **4** 電鑽
brace **5** 曲柄鑽
bit **6** 鑽頭
axe **7** 斧頭
bolt **8** 帶帽螺絲釘
screw **9** 螺絲釘
thread **10** 螺紋

nail **11** 釘
washer **12** 墊圈
nut **13** 螺絲帽
hammer **14** 錘
head **15** 頭
handle **16** 柄
saw **17** 鋸
hacksaw **18** 弓背鋸
pliers **19** 密嘴鉗

roof	**1**	屋頂	shutter	**12**	百葉窗
chimney	**2**	煙囪	window-box	**13**	花槽
wall	**3**	牆壁	curtain	**14**	窗簾
balcony	**4**	露台，陽台	blind	**15**	窗簾
patio	**5**	天井	gutter	**16**	檐溝
garage	**6**	車房	drainpipe	**17**	排水管
(front) door	**7**	（前）門	doormat	**18**	門前地墊
window	**8**	窗	aerial	**19**	天綫
window-frame	**9**	窗框	(garden-)shed	**20**	工具房
window-pane	**10**	窗格玻璃	grass	**21**	草
(window-)ledge/sill	**11**	窗台			

The Weather	天氣		twigs 14	細樹枝
lightning 1	閃電		leaves 15	樹葉
(storm-/thunder-) 2	（暴風）雲		gate 16	柵門
cloud			hedge 17	樹籬
rain 3	雨		path 18	小徑
raindrops 4	雨點		lawn 19	草地
snow 5	雪		flower 20	花
snowball 6	雪球		flower-bed 21	花床，花圃
snowman 7	雪人		shrub/bush 22	灌木，矮樹
icicle 8	冰柱		watering-can 23	澆水壺
sun 9	太陽		flower-pot 24	花盆
sky 10	天空		(garden-)fork 25	草叉
			shed 26	工具房
In the Garden	在花園		wheelbarrow 27	獨輪車
tree 11	樹		washing line 28	晾衣繩
trunk 12	樹幹		washing 29	洗淨的衣物
branch 13	樹枝		(clothes-)peg 30	（晾衣）夾

door	**1**	門	stair	**16**	梯級
(door-)knocker	**2**	（扣門）門環	staircase	**17**	樓梯
(door-)bell	**3**	（門）鈴	banister	**18**	欄干
doorstep	**4**	台階	handrail	**19**	扶手
letter-box	**5**	信箱	upstairs	**20**	上樓梯
keyhole	**6**	匙孔	downstairs	**21**	下樓梯
lock and chain	**7**	鎖和門鏈	light	**22**	燈
bolt	**8**	門閂	(light-)switch	**23**	（燈）開關
hinge	**9**	鉸鏈	clock	**24**	鐘
(door)mat	**10**	（門前）地墊	telephone/phone	**25**	電話
floor	**11**	地板	receiver	**26**	聽筒
rug	**12**	地毯	dial	**27**	撥號碼盤
(coat) rack	**13**	（掛大衣）架	cord/flex	**28**	電綫
peg	**14**	掛鈎	(tele)phone	**29**	電話簿
key	**15**	鑰匙	directory/book		

ceiling	**1**	天花板	radio **22**	收音機
wall	**2**	牆	(dining-)table **23**	餐枱
carpet	**3**	地毯	chair **24**	椅
fireplace	**4**	火爐，壁爐	table-mat **25**	餐墊
mantelpiece	**5**	壁爐台	fork **26**	叉
fire	**6**	火	spoon **27**	匙
curtain	**7**	窗簾	knife **28**	刀
armchair	**8**	靠手椅	glass **29**	玻璃杯
cushion	**9**	椅墊	cup **30**	杯
bookcase	**10**	書架	saucer **31**	茶杯碟
record-player	**11**	電唱機	butter-dish **32**	牛油碟
picture	**12**	（圖）畫	coffee-pot **33**	咖啡壺
frame	**13**	畫框	spout **34**	壺嘴
vase of flowers	**14**	一瓶花	lid **35**	蓋
lamp	**15**	座燈	teapot **36**	茶壺
lampshade	**16**	燈罩	(milk-)jug **37**	（牛奶）壺
television/TV	**17**	電視機	handle **38**	柄，把手
(television) screen	**18**	（電視）熒光幕	(sugar-)bowl **39**	（糖）缸
coffee-table	**19**	咖啡几	bread-board **40**	切麵飽板
record	**20**	唱片	bread-knife **41**	麵飽刀
couch/settee/sofa	**21**	長沙發		

cooker/stove	**1**	爐	rolling-pin	**18**	擀麵杖
oven	**2**	焗爐	(cake-)tin	**19**	（餅）罐
grill	**3**	烤架	jug	**20**	壺
ring	**4**	爐環	tin-opener	**21**	罐頭刀
refrigerator/fridge	**5**	電冰箱，雪櫃	tin/can	**22**	罐頭
larder	**6**	廚櫃	basket	**23**	籃子
sink	**7**	洗碗盆	cookery book	**24**	食譜
draining-board	**8**	滴水板	colander	**25**	濾盆
rubbish-bin	**9**	垃圾桶	scourer	**26**	洗擦器
vegetable-rack	**10**	蔬菜架	washing-up brush	**27**	洗碗刷
frying-pan	**11**	平底鍋，煎鍋	washing-up liquid	**28**	洗潔精
pot/(sauce)pan	**12**	鍋	dish-cloth	**29**	碗布
kettle	**13**	燒水壺	sieve/strainer	**30**	篩
tray	**14**	托盤	ladle	**31**	長柄勺
bread-bin	**15**	麵飽盒	tea-towel/drying-up	**32**	茶杯布
shelf	**16**	攔板	cloth		
(kitchen) scales	**17**	（廚房用的）磅			

vacuum-cleaner/hoover	**1**	吸塵機	scrubbing-brush	**10**	硬毛刷
broom	**2**	掃帚	iron	**11**	熨斗
ironing-board	**3**	熨衣板	flex	**12**	電綫
washing-machine	**4**	洗衣機	(light-)bulb	**13**	電燈泡
mop	**5**	地拖	hairdrier	**14**	乾髮器
brush	**6**	刷子	plug	**15**	（電）插頭
duster	**7**	抹布	socket/power-point	**16**	（電）插座
dustpan	**8**	畚箕	switch	**17**	開關
scouring powder	**9**	洗擦粉	soap powder	**18**	洗衣粉
			bucket	**19**	水桶

The Bedroom	睡房	(hair)brush **20**	（髮）刷，（頭）刷
bed **1**	牀	comb **21**	梳
headboard **2**	牀頭屏	box of tissues **22**	一盒紙巾
pillow **3**	枕頭	jewellery box **23**	手飾箱
pillow-case/-slip **4**	枕套	(alarm-)clock **24**	鬧鐘
sheet **5**	牀單	lamp **25**	枱燈
blanket **6**	（毛）氈		
bedspread **7**	牀罩	**Baby**	嬰兒
mattress **8**	牀褥，牀墊	cot **26**	嬰兒牀
bedside table **9**	牀頭小桌	sleeping suit **27**	全身睡衣
dressing-table **10**	梳妝台	dummy **28**	橡皮奶頭，奶嘴
stool **11**	櫈子	teddy-bear **29**	玩具熊
mirror **12**	鏡	rattle **30**	敲擊發聲的玩具
cupboard **13**	櫥櫃	doll **31**	玩偶，洋娃娃
wardrobe **14**	衣櫃	potty **32**	便罐，尿壺
chest-of-drawers **15**	抽屜櫃	bottle **33**	奶瓶
rug **16**	地毯	teat **34**	奶嘴
clothes **17**	衣服	bib **35**	涎布，圍涎
clothes-brush **18**	衣刷	nappy **36**	尿布
(coat-)hanger **19**	衣架		

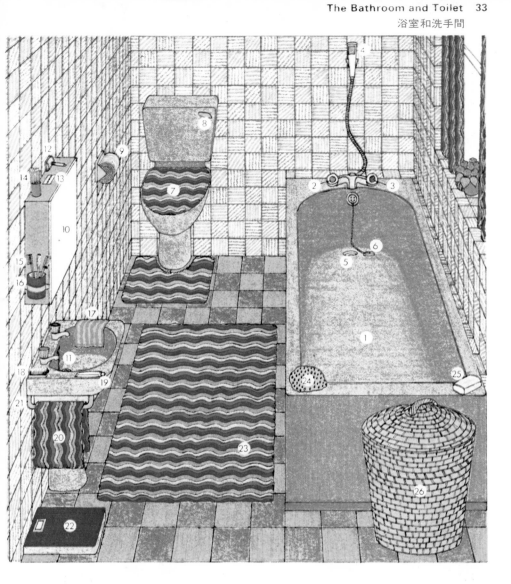

bath	1	浴缸	shaving-brush	14	修臉刷
hot(-water) tap	2	熱水龍頭	toothbrush	15	牙刷
cold(-water) tap	3	冷水龍頭	toothmug	16	漱口缸
shower	4	蓮蓬頭，花灑	(face-)flannel	17	（面）巾
plug-hole	5	排水孔	nailbrush	18	指甲刷
plug	6	塞（子）	(tube of) toothpaste	19	（一管）牙膏
toilet/lavatory/loo	7	厠所	towel	20	毛巾
handle	8	冲水手掣	towel-rail	21	毛巾架
toilet-roll/toilet-	9	衛生紙，厠紙	(bathroom) scales	22	（浴室）磅
paper/lavatory-paper			bathmat	23	浴室地墊
bathroom cabinet	10	盥洗用品櫥	sponge	24	海綿
(wash-)basin	11	洗臉盆，洗手盆	soap	25	肥皂
razor	12	刮臉刀	laundry-basket	26	裝載待洗衣物的籃子
(razor) blade	13	刀片			

plateau	**1**	高原	meadow	**11**	草原，草地
mountain	**2**	山	river	**12**	河流
(mountain) peak	**3**	山峰，山頂	field	**13**	田
waterfall	**4**	瀑布	hedge	**14**	樹籬
lake	**5**	湖	tree	**15**	樹
valley	**6**	山谷	village	**16**	鄉村
stream	**7**	小河	(foot)path	**17**	小徑
wood	**8**	樹林	road	**18**	路
forest	**9**	森林	pond	**19**	池塘
hill	**10**	小山丘			

Camping		露營
tent	1	帳幕
groundsheet	2	鋪在地上的防潮布
sleeping-bag	3	睡袋
rucksack	4	背囊
camping stove	5	露營用的爐
At the seaside		在海濱
cliff	6	懸崖
hotel	7	酒店
bungalow/chalet	8	平房
promenade/sea-front	9	海濱大道
sea-wall	10	防波堤
beach	11	沙灘，海灘
sunshade	12	太陽傘
sunbather	13	日光浴者
(beach-)towel	14	（沙灘）毛巾
mask/goggles	15	面罩／護目鏡
snorkel	16	（潛泳者的）通氣管
ice-cream	17	冰淇淋，雪糕
windbreak	18	防風帳
deckchair	19	躺椅
swimming/bathing trunks	20	游泳褲
flipper	21	橡皮腳掌，蛙鞋
sand	22	沙
sandcastle	23	沙堆的堡壘
bucket	24	桶
spade	25	鏟
beachball	26	沙灘球
shell	27	貝殼
pebbles	28	卵石
rocks	29	石頭
kite	30	風箏
sea	31	海
surf	32	浪花
wave	33	波浪
motor-boat	34	摩托船，汽船
swimmer	35	游泳者
swimming-/bathing-costume	36	游泳衣
seaweed	37	海草，海藻

hayloft	**1**	乾草頂棚	plough **19**	犁
hay	**2**	乾草	furrow **20**	犁溝
cowshed	**3**	牛棚	cow **21**	母牛，奶牛
barn	**4**	穀倉	calf **22**	小牛
pen	**5**	家畜的欄	bull **23**	公牛
farmyard	**6**	農場內的院子	goats **24**	山羊
farmhouse	**7**	農場內的住房	beehive **25**	蜂房，蜂箱
field	**8**	田	shepherd **26**	牧羊人
pond	**9**	池塘	crook **27**	彎柄杖
fence	**10**	柵欄	sheepdog **28**	牧羊狗
fruit-tree	**11**	果樹	sheep **29**	羊
orchard	**12**	果園	lamb **30**	小羊
scarecrow	**13**	稻草人	duckling **31**	小鴨
wheat	**14**	小麥	duck **32**	鴨
farmer	**15**	農人	hen/chicken **33**	母雞
combine harvester	**16**	聯合收割機	cock **34**	公雞
irrigation canal	**17**	灌溉渠	chick **35**	小雞
tractor	**18**	拖拉機		

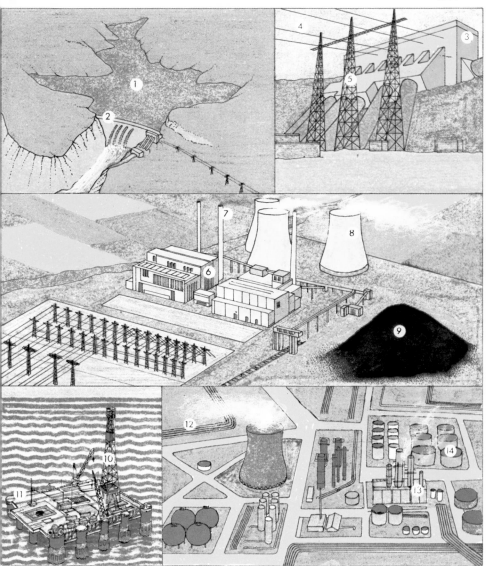

reservoir	**1**	水庫，水塘	cooling tower	**8**	冷却塔
dam	**2**	水塢	fuel	**9**	燃料
power-house	**3**	發電廠	oil-derrick	**10**	油井鐵架
cable	**4**	電纜	oil-rig	**11**	鑽井機
pylon	**5**	架高壓電纜的鐵架	pipeline	**12**	輸油管
power station	**6**	發電站	refinery	**13**	煉油廠
chimney	**7**	煙囱	storage tank	**14**	貯油庫，貯油桶

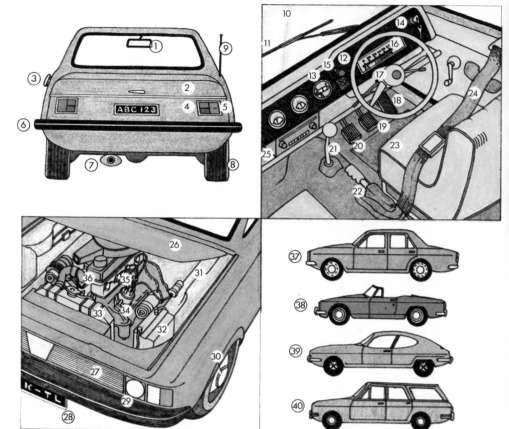

The (motor-)car		汽車
rear-mirror	**1**	望後鏡
boot	**2**	行李箱
petrol-cap	**3**	油箱蓋
rear-light	**4**	後燈
indicator (light)	**5**	指示燈
bumper	**6**	保險槓
exhaust(-pipe)	**7**	排氣管
tyre	**8**	車輪
aerial	**9**	天綫
windscreen	**10**	擋風玻璃
windscreen-wiper	**11**	刮水器，水撥
dashboard	**12**	儀器板，錶板
petrol gauge	**13**	油壓錶
ignition	**14**	發火
choke	**15**	阻塞門
speedometer	**16**	速度計，咪錶
steering-wheel	**17**	駕駛盤
accelerator	**18**	加速器
(foot)brake	**19**	（脚）煞車掣
clutch	**20**	離合器
gear-lever	**21**	排檔桿，變速桿
(hand)brake	**22**	（手）掣
seat	**23**	座位
seat-/safety-belt	**24**	安全帶
car radio	**25**	汽車收音機
bonnet	**26**	引擎蓋
radiator grill	**27**	水箱護柵
number-plate	**28**	號碼牌
headlight	**29**	前燈
hubcap	**30**	輪轂蓋
engine	**31**	引擎
battery	**32**	電池
radiator	**33**	水箱，冷却器
distributor	**34**	配電盤
sparking-plug	**35**	火花塞
cylinder-head	**36**	汽缸蓋
saloon	**37**	大轎車
convertible	**38**	開蓬汽車
coupé	**39**	單門轎車
estate	**40**	客貨兩用轎車

motorway	**1**	高速公路	transporter **12**	運載汽車的卡車
fly-over	**2**	天橋	caravan **13**	蓬車
underpass	**3**	橋下通道	lorry **14**	貨車
roundabout	**4**	迴旋處	ambulance **15**	救護車
outside lane	**5**	外行車綫	car **16**	汽車
inside lane	**6**	內行車綫	coach **17**	長途公共汽車
petrol-/service- station	**7**	汽油站	sportscar **18**	跑車
petrol-pump	**8**	汽油泵	tanker **19**	油槽車
air-pump	**9**	氣泵	motorbike/cycle **20**	摩托車，電單車
attendant	**10**	服務員	trailer **21**	拖車
articulated lorry	**11**	鉸接拖車	van **22**	小型貨車，行李車

陸上旅行（三）

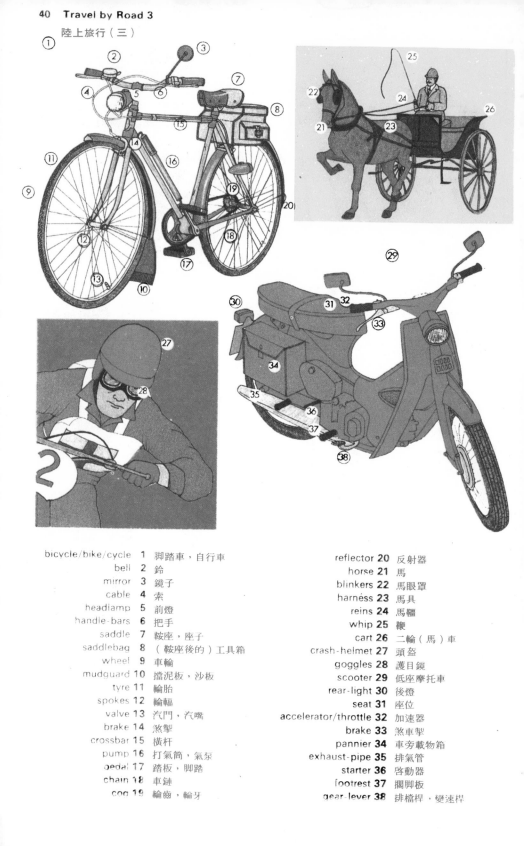

bicycle/bike/cycle	1	脚踏車，自行車	reflector	20	反射器
bell	2	鈴	horse	21	馬
mirror	3	鏡子	blinkers	22	馬眼罩
cable	4	索	harness	23	馬具
headlamp	5	前燈	reins	24	馬韁
handle-bars	6	把手	whip	25	鞭
saddle	7	鞍座，座子	cart	26	二輪（馬）車
saddlebag	8	（鞍座後的）工具箱	crash-helmet	27	頭盔
wheel	9	車輪	goggles	28	護目鏡
mudguard	10	擋泥板，沙板	scooter	29	低座摩托車
tyre	11	輪胎	rear-light	30	後燈
spokes	12	輪輻	seat	31	座位
valve	13	汽門，汽嘴	accelerator/throttle	32	加速器
brake	14	煞掣	brake	33	煞車掣
crossbar	15	橫桿	pannier	34	車旁載物箱
pump	16	打氣筒，氣泵	exhaust-pipe	35	排氣管
pedal	17	踏板，脚踏	starter	36	啓動器
chain	18	車鏈	footrest	37	擱脚板
cog	19	輪齒，輪牙	gear-lever	38	排檔桿，變速桿

train	1	火車	barrier	17	柵欄
driver	2	司機	waiting-room	18	候車室
engine	3	火車頭，機車	passengers	19	乘客
coach	4	車廂	platform	20	月台
compartment	5	車室	platform number	21	月台號碼
(ticket-)inspector	6	查票員	signalman	22	訊號員
ticket	7	車票	signal-box	23	訊號所
seat	8	座位	railway-line	24	火車軌，鐵軌
luggage-rack	9	行李架	sleepers	25	枕木
guard	10	列車員	points	26	轉轍器，道閘
flag	11	旗	signals	27	訊號
whistle	12	哨子	goods-truck, waggon	28	貨卡
station	13	火車站	buffer	29	緩衝器
ticket-office	14	售票處	siding	30	旁軌
timetable	15	行車時間表			
ticket-collector	16	收票員			

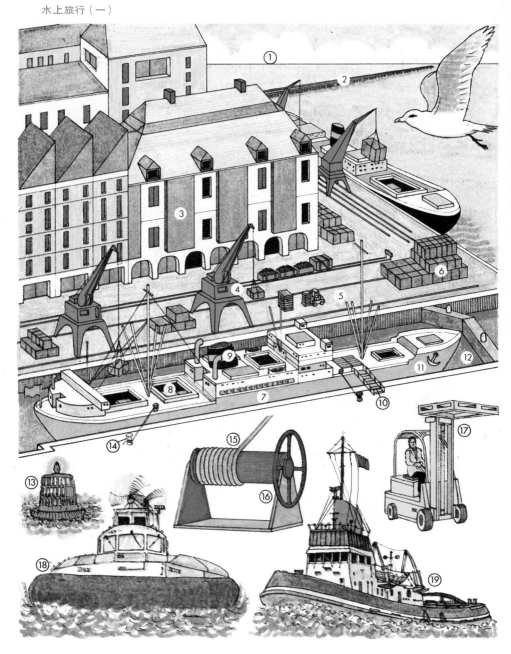

horizon	1	地平綫	anchor 11	錨
pier	2	防波堤	dock 12	船塢
warehouse	3	貨倉	buoy 13	浮標
crane	4	起重機	bollard 14	繫纜柱
wharf/quay	5	碼頭	cable 15	纜
cargo	6	貨物	windlass 16	起錨機
ship	7	船	fork-lift truck 17	叉式裝卸車
hold	8	底艙	hovercraft 18	氣墊船
funnel	9	煙囱	tug 19	拖船
gangway	10	舷梯，跳板		

yacht	**1**	遊艇	motor-boat/-launch	**12**	摩托船，汽船
(cabin-)cruiser	**2**	帶客艙遊艇	outboard motor	**13**	艇外推進器
mast	**3**	船桅	propeller	**14**	螺旋槳
sail	**4**	帆	ferry	**15**	渡船
junk	**5**	帆船	barge	**16**	駁船
rowing-boat	**6**	舢板	trawler	**17**	拖網漁船
oar	**7**	槳	(oil-)tanker	**18**	油船
canoe	**8**	獨木舟	deck	**19**	甲板
paddle	**9**	槳	liner	**20**	郵船，客船
punt	**10**	方頭平底船	funnel	**21**	煙囪
pole	**11**	撐篙			

customs hall	1	海關處	jet engine 12	噴射引擎
customs officer	2	海關官員	(tail)fin 13	機尾
passport	3	護照	glider 14	滑翔機
luggage baggage	4	行李	helicopter 15	直升機
captain	5	機長	rotor 16	旋翼
passenger	6	搭客	light aircraft 17	輕便飛機
air-hostess	7	飛機女服務員	propeller 18	螺旋槳
air steward	8	飛機男服務員	runway 19	跑道
(aero)plane airliner	9	飛機	control tower 20	指揮塔
fuselage	10	機身	hangar 21	飛機庫
wing	11	機翼		

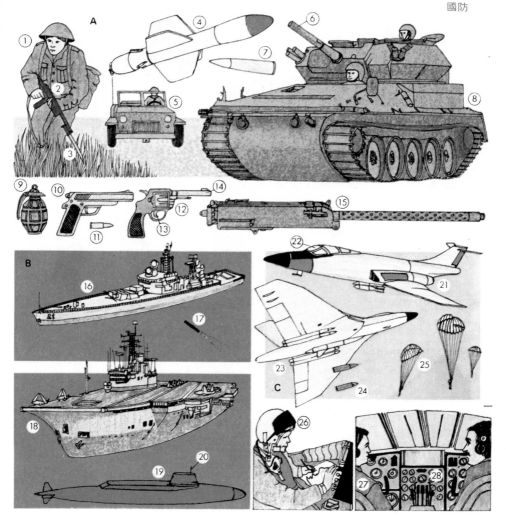

Army A.		陸軍	**Navy B.**		海軍
soldier	**1**	軍人，士兵	warship	**16**	軍艦，戰艦
rifle	**2**	來福槍，步槍	torpedo	**17**	魚雷
bayonet	**3**	刺刀	aircraft-carrier	**18**	航空母艦
guided missile	**4**	導向飛彈	submarine	**19**	潛（水）艇
jeep	**5**	吉普車	periscope	**20**	潛望鏡
gun	**6**	砲			
shell	**7**	砲彈	**Air Force C.**		空軍
tank	**8**	坦克，戰車	fighter plane	**21**	戰鬥機
(hand-)grenade	**9**	手榴彈	cockpit	**22**	座艙
pistol	**10**	手槍	bomber	**23**	轟炸機
bullet/cartridge	**11**	子彈	bomb	**24**	炸彈
revolver	**12**	左輪手槍	parachute	**25**	降落傘
trigger	**13**	扳機	navigator	**26**	領航員
barrel	**14**	槍管	pilot	**27**	駕駛員
machine-gun	**15**	機關槍	control-panel	**28**	控制台

(Horse-)racing A.	賽馬	backboard **16**	籃板
jockey **1**	騎師	ball **17**	球
(race-)horse **2**	（比賽的）馬		
saddle **3**	馬鞍	**Hockey D.**	曲棍球
reins **4**	馬韁	stick **18**	球棍
bridle **5**	轡頭		
bit **6**	嚼子	**Table-tennis E.**	乒乓球
stirrup **7**	馬鐙	bat **19**	球拍
riding breeches/ **8**	馬褲	net **20**	球網
jodhpurs		table **21**	球桌
cap **9**	帽		
		Wrestling F.	摔角
Boxing B.	拳擊	wrestlers **22**	摔角手
referee **10**	裁判員		
boxer **11**	拳擊員	**Judo G.**	柔道
glove **12**	拳擊手套	judo suit **23**	柔道袍
ring **13**	拳擊場		
ropes **14**	圍繩	**Rugby H.**	（橄）欖球
		player **24**	球手
Basketball C.	籃球	goal **25**	球門
basket **15**	籃		

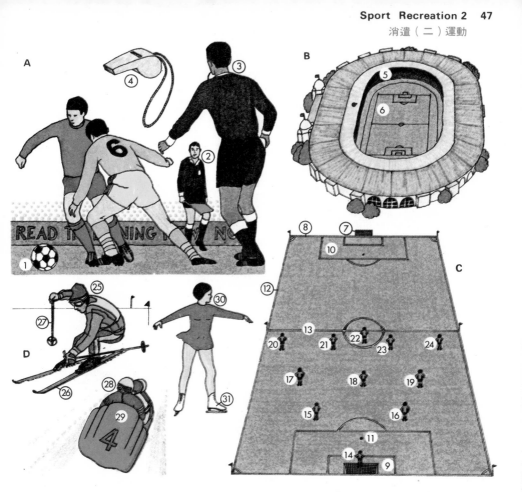

Football/Soccer A.		足球
(foot)ball	**1**	足球
linesman	**2**	旁證，巡邊員
referee	**3**	球證，裁判員
whistle	**4**	哨子
Stadium B.		運動場
stand	**5**	看台
pitch/field	**6**	場地
Line-up C.		整隊
goal	**7**	球門
goal-line	**8**	底綫
goal area	**9**	球門區
penalty area	**10**	禁區
penalty spot	**11**	罰球點
touch line	**12**	橫邊
halfway line	**13**	中綫
goalkeeper	**14**	守門員
defenders { left back	**15**	左後衞 } 後防球員
right back	**16**	右後衞

midfield players {	left half	**17**	左中衞 } 中場球員
	centre half	**18**	中衞
	right half	**19**	右中衞
strikers {	outside left	**20**	左翼 } 攻擊球員 (前鋒)
	inside left	**21**	左輔
	centre forward	**22**	中鋒
	inside right	**23**	右輔
	outside right	**24**	右翼

Winter Sports D.		冬季運動
skier	**25**	滑雪者
ski	**26**	滑雪履
(ski-)stick/pole	**27**	滑雪桿
tobogganist	**28**	滑平底雪橇者
toboggan	**29**	平底雪橇
skater	**30**	溜冰者
skate	**31**	溜冰鞋

Baseball A		棒球
catcher	**1**	捕手
mask	**2**	面罩
glove	**3**	手套
bat	**4**	球棒
batter	**5**	擊球員
Cricket B.		板球
batsman	**6**	擊球手
bat	**7**	球棒
bails	**8**	（三柱門上的）橫木
wicket/stumps	**9**	三柱門
cricket ball	**10**	板球
wicket-keeper	**11**	守門員
pad	**12**	護墊
pitch	**13**	場地
bowler	**14**	投手
fielder	**15**	外場隊員

umpire	**16**	裁判員
crease	**17**	（投手的）界限綫
Fishing C.		釣魚
fisherman	**18**	釣魚者
rod	**19**	魚竿
line	**20**	魚絲
hook	**21**	鈎
bait	**22**	餌
Tennis D.		網球
(tennis-)court	**23**	（網）球場
net	**24**	網
server	**25**	發球者
service line	**26**	發球界綫
racket	**27**	球拍
tennis-ball	**28**	網球

Orchestra		樂隊
flute	**1**	長笛
clarinet	**2**	單簧管
musician/player	**3**	音樂家，樂師
violin	**4**	小提琴
strings	**5**	弦
bow	**6**	弓
viola	**7**	中提琴
cello	**8**	大提琴
double-bass	**9**	低音提琴
conductor	**10**	指揮
baton	**11**	指揮棒
(sheet) music	**12**	樂譜
rostrum	**13**	壇
horn	**14**	號角
piano	**15**	鋼琴
keys	**16**	琴鍵

pedal	**17**	踏板
stool	**18**	橙
trumpet	**19**	小號，喇叭
trombone	**20**	伸縮喇叭
slide	**21**	U形伸縮管
saxophone	**22**	薩克斯管
mouthpiece	**23**	吹口

Pop Group		流行樂隊
singer	**24**	歌手
microphone/mike	**25**	麥克風
(electric) guitar	**26**	（電）結他
amplifier	**27**	擴音器
loudspeaker	**28**	揚聲器
cymbals	**29**	鐃鈸
drum	**30**	鼓

The Theatre A.	戲院，劇院	
stage	**1**	舞台
actor	**2**	男演員
actress	**3**	女演員
set	**4**	佈景
wings	**5**	側景
curtain	**6**	幕
spotlight	**7**	聚光燈
theatre	**8**	戲院，劇院
gallery	**9**	高座
circle/balcony	**10**	樓座
stalls	**11**	前後座
(orchestra) pit	**12**	樂池
footlights	**13**	腳燈

The Cinema B.	電影院	
projection room	**14**	放映室
projector	**15**	放映機
projectionist	**16**	放映員
cinema	**17**	電影院
screen	**18**	銀幕
usherette	**19**	女引座員
seats	**20**	座位
aisle/gangway	**21**	過道，走廊

The Library C.	圖書館	
librarian	**22**	圖書管理員
card-index	**23**	圖書索引
counter/desk	**24**	櫃枱
bookshelf	**25**	書架

(beer-)bottle	**1**	（啤酒）瓶
bottle-top	**2**	瓶蓋
beer-mug	**3**	啤酒杯
(beer-)can	**4**	（啤酒）罐
matchbox	**5**	火柴盒
match	**6**	火柴
bottle-opener	**7**	開瓶刀
cigarette	**8**	香煙
ash	**9**	煙灰
ashtray	**10**	煙灰碟，煙灰缸
corkscrew	**11**	瓶塞鑽
straw	**12**	飲管
soft drink	**13**	飲品
tankard	**14**	銀或錫鑞製的大酒杯
juke-box	**15**	自動點唱機
bar	**16**	酒吧
barmaid	**17**	酒吧間女招待員
barman	**18**	酒吧間男招待員
pump	**19**	酒泵
(bar-)stool	**20**	（酒吧）高櫈
waiter	**21**	服務員，侍應生
customer	**22**	顧客
menu	**23**	菜單
bottle of wine	**24**	一瓶酒
cork	**25**	瓶塞
(wine-)glass	**26**	（酒）杯
salt(-cellar)	**27**	鹽（瓶）
mustard(-pot)	**28**	芥末（瓶）
pepper(-pot)	**29**	胡椒（瓶）
table-cloth	**30**	枱布
napkin/serviette	**31**	餐巾

Chess and Draughts A.	國際象棋和西洋跳棋	**Reading C.**	閱讀
(set of) chessmen **1**	（一副）棋子	book **15**	書本
chess pieces		cover **16**	封面
board **2**	棋盤	(dust-)jacket **17**	護封
pawn **3**	兵，卒	spine **18**	書脊
rook/castle **4**	堡壘（相當於中國象棋的車）	page **19**	頁
knight **5**	武士（相當於中國象棋的馬）	illustration **20**	插圖
bishop **6**	主教（相當於中國象棋的象或相）	text **21**	原文，本文
queen **7**	后		
king **8**	王（相當於中國象棋的將或帥）	**Photography D.**	攝影
draughts **9**	西洋跳棋	print/photograph/ **22**	照片，相片
		photo/snapshot	
Cards B.	紙牌	negative **23**	底片
(pack of) **10**	（一副）紙牌	(roll of) film **24**	（一卷）軟片
(playing-)cards		camera **25**	攝影機
jack/knave of clubs **11**	梅花王子	lens **26**	鏡頭
queen of diamonds **12**	鑽石王后	screen **27**	銀幕
king of hearts **13**	紅心王	stand **28**	支架
ace of spades **14**	黑桃么點	(slide-)projector **29**	（幻燈）放映機
		slide **30**	幻燈片

sewing-machine	**1**	縫紉機，衣車	button	**15**	鈕扣
tape	**2**	綫帶	button-hole	**16**	鈕門，鈕孔
seam	**3**	接縫	stitch	**17**	針步
hem	**4**	折邊	knitting-needle	**18**	織針
thimble	**5**	頂針	wool	**19**	毛綫，毛冷
needle	**6**	針	pattern	**20**	（編織）圖案
elastic	**7**	橡筋帶	knitting	**21**	編織
reel of cotton	**8**	綫軸	zip/zipper/zip-	**22**	拉鍊
lace	**9**	花邊	fastener		
safety-pin	**10**	別針	hook and eye	**23**	扣和扣眼
pleat	**11**	褶	ribbon	**24**	絲帶
pin	**12**	別針，大頭針	tape-measure	**25**	軟尺
material/cloth	**13**	布料	scissors	**26**	剪刀
frill	**14**	褶邊，飾邊	press-stud	**27**	按扣

職業（一）

hairdresser **1** 理髮師	typist **9** 打字員	
butcher **2** 肉店售貨員	dressmaker **10** 女服裁縫	
carpenter **3** 木匠	waitress **11** 女服務員，女侍應生	
bank-clerk **4** 銀行職員	driver **12** 司機	
mechanic **5** 機械工人	clown **13** 小丑	
docker **6** 船塢工人	porter **14** 行李搬運工人	
miner **7** 礦工	announcer **15** 播音員	
artist **8** 藝術家		

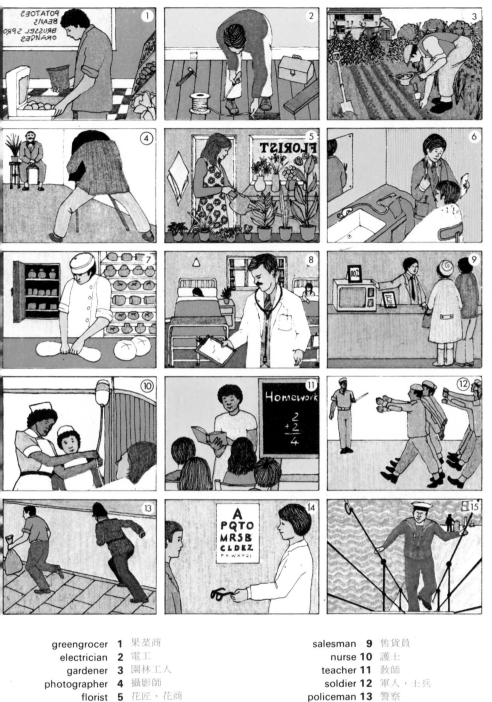

greengrocer	**1**	果菜商
electrician	**2**	電工
gardener	**3**	園林工人
photographer	**4**	攝影師
florist	**5**	花匠，花商
barber	**6**	理髮師
baker	**7**	麵飽師
doctor	**8**	醫生
salesman	**9**	售貨員
nurse	**10**	護士
teacher	**11**	教師
soldier	**12**	軍人，士兵
policeman	**13**	警察
optician	**14**	驗眼師，眼鏡商
sailor	**15**	水手，海員

horse	**1**	馬
foal	**2**	駒
pig	**3**	豬
snout	**4**	口鼻部
llama	**5**	美洲駝，無峰駝
camel	**6**	駱駝
hump	**7**	駝峰
buffalo	**8**	水牛
horn	**9**	角
donkey	**10**	驢
reindeer	**11**	馴鹿
antler	**12**	鹿角
dog	**13**	狗

puppy	**14**	小狗
cat	**15**	貓
kitten	**16**	小貓
paw	**17**	爪
mouse	**18**	鼠
squirrel	**19**	松鼠
rabbit	**20**	兔
whisker	**21**	鬚
rat	**22**	鼠
tail	**23**	尾巴
fox	**24**	狐狸
bat	**25**	蝙蝠
hedgehog	**26**	刺猬

whale	1	鯨魚	gorilla	14	大猩猩
fluke	2	鯨魚尾鰭	giraffe	15	長頸鹿
dolphin	3	海豚	lion	16	獅子
fin	4	鰭，翅	mane	17	鬃毛
antelope	5	羚羊	leopard	18	豹
kangaroo	6	袋鼠	tiger	19	老虎
pouch	7	袋	hippopotamus	20	河馬
bear	8	熊	elephant	21	大象
seal	9	海豹	trunk	22	象鼻
flipper	10	闊鰭	tusk	23	象牙
wolf	11	狼	zebra	24	斑馬
baboon	12	狒狒	rhinoceros	25	犀牛
monkey	13	猴子	horn	26	角

Fish and other animals	魚類及其他動物		shell	**14**	殼
shark	**1**	鯊魚	sunfish	**15**	翻車魚
fin	**2**	鰭，翅	oyster	**16**	蠔
swordfish	**3**	旗魚	crab	**17**	蟹
salmon	**4**	鮭魚，三文魚	pincer/claw	**18**	螯
gill	**5**	鰓	slug	**19**	蛞蝓
herring	**6**	鯡魚，青魚	frog	**20**	青蛙
tail	**7**	魚尾	worm	**21**	蚯蚓
snout	**8**	口鼻部	centipede	**22**	蜈蚣
scales	**9**	魚鱗	octopus	**23**	鱆魚
eel	**10**	鰻，鱔	tentacle	**24**	觸手，觸鬚
jelly-fish	**11**	水母	spider	**25**	蜘蛛
lobster	**12**	龍蝦	(cob)web	**26**	蜘蛛網
snail	**13**	蝸牛	scorpion	**27**	蠍子

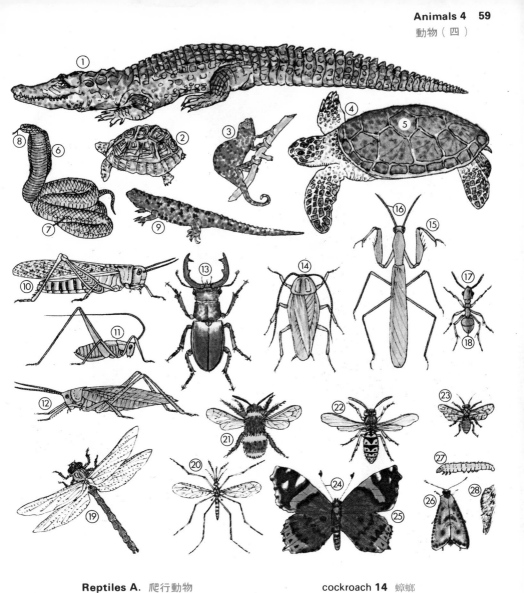

Reptiles A.	爬行動物	cockroach **14**	蟑螂
crocodile **1**	鱷魚	mantis **15**	螳螂
tortoise **2**	龜	feeler **16**	觸角
chameleon **3**	變色蜥蜴	ant **17**	螞蟻
turtle **4**	海龜	abdomen **18**	腹部
shell **5**	殼	dragonfly **19**	蜻蜓
snake **6**	蛇	mosquito **20**	蚊
coil **7**	盤繞	bee **21**	蜜蜂
tongue **8**	舌頭	wasp **22**	黃蜂
lizard **9**	蜥蜴	fly **23**	蒼蠅
		antenna **24**	觸角
Insects B.	昆蟲類	butterfly **25**	蝴蝶
locust **10**	蝗蟲	moth **26**	蛾
cricket **11**	蟋蟀	caterpillar **27**	毛蟲
grasshopper **12**	蚱蜢	cocoon **28**	繭
beetle **13**	甲蟲		

Animals 5
動物（五）

Birds		鳥類
ostrich	**1**	鴕鳥
eagle	**2**	鷹
claw	**3**	爪
beak	**4**	鳥嘴，喙
feathers	**5**	羽毛
hawk	**6**	鵰
owl	**7**	貓頭鷹
flamingo	**8**	紅鶴
webbed foot	**9**	有蹼的足
vulture	**10**	兀鷲
peacock	**11**	孔雀
crest	**12**	冠
penguin	**13**	企鵝
pheasant	**14**	雉，野雞
heron	**15**	鷺
turkey	**16**	火雞
swan	**17**	天鵝
canary	**18**	金絲雀
bill	**19**	細長扁平的嘴
parrot	**20**	鸚鵡
(sea)gull	**21**	海鷗
swallow	**22**	燕子
wing	**23**	翼
dove	**24**	鴿子
goose	**25**	鵝
budgerigar	**26**	長尾鸚鵡
humming-bird	**27**	蜂鳥
sparrow	**28**	麻雀
nest	**29**	巢
kingfisher	**30**	翠鳥
pigeon	**31**	家鴿
blackbird	**32**	畫眉
crow	**33**	烏鴉

Fruit		果類	peel/rind	**18**	果皮
apple	**1**	蘋果	peach	**19**	桃
stalk	**2**	莖	stone	**20**	核，種子
skin	**3**	皮	strawberry	**21**	草莓
core	**4**	果心	pear	**22**	梨
banana	**5**	香蕉	plum	**23**	梅
peel	**6**	果皮	pineapple	**24**	菠蘿，鳳梨
cherry	**7**	櫻桃	pawpaw/papaya	**25**	木瓜
stone	**8**	核，種子	lychee	**26**	荔枝
coconut	**9**	椰子	walnut	**27**	合桃
date	**10**	棗	kernel	**28**	核，仁
peanut/groundnut	**11**	花生	fig	**29**	無花果
grapes	**12**	葡萄	grapefruit	**30**	西印度柚
vine	**13**	葡萄樹			
lemon	**14**	檸檬	cactus	**31**	仙人掌
mango	**15**	芒果	fern	**32**	蕨
orange	**16**	橙	frond	**33**	複葉
segments	**17**	瓣			

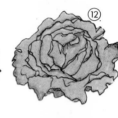

Vegetables		蔬菜
bean	1	豆
stalk	2	莖，葉柄
pea	3	豌豆
pod	4	莢
carrot	5	胡蘿蔔，紅蘿蔔
potato	6	馬鈴薯
marrow	7	胡蘆科的瓜類
cucumber	8	青瓜，黃瓜
beetroot	9	甜菜根，紅菜頭
cauliflower	10	椰菜花
cabbage	11	椰菜
lettuce	12	萵苣，生菜
onion	13	洋葱
mushroom	14	蘑菇，菌
tomato	15	番茄，西紅柿
aubergine/eggplant	16	茄子

Flowers		花卉
daffodil	17	水仙
daisy	18	雛菊
rose	19	玫瑰
petal	20	花瓣
orchid	21	蘭
tulip	22	鬱金香
stem	23	莖
hibiscus	24	大紅花
bud	25	蓓蕾
waterlily	26	睡蓮
sunflower	27	向日葵
seeds	28	種子

corn/maize	**1**	玉蜀黍，玉米	branch/bough **13**	樹枝
ear of wheat	**2**	麥穗	twig **14**	小樹枝
olive	**3**	橄欖	leaf **15**	葉
cocoa pod	**4**	可可莢	acorn **16**	橡樹果
coffee berry	**5**	咖啡豆	bark **17**	樹皮
cotton	**6**	棉花	log **18**	圓木
rice	**7**	米	palm **19**	棕櫚樹
tea	**8**	茶	fir **20**	杉樹
sugar-cane	**9**	甘蔗	cone **21**	球果
oak tree	**10**	橡樹	needles **22**	針葉
roots	**11**	根	cedar **23**	雪松
trunk	**12**	樹幹	willow **24**	柳樹

blow	**1**	吹
break	**2**	折斷
carry	**3**	手提
catch	**4**	接
climb	**5**	攀登
crawl	**6**	爬行
cry/weep	**7**	哭泣
cut	**8**	剪
dance	**9**	跳舞
dig	**10**	挖掘
dive	**11**	跳水
draw	**12**	繪畫
drink	**13**	飲
dream	**14**	做夢
drive	**15**	駕駛
drown	**16**	沉溺
eat	**17**	吃，食
fall	**18**	跌倒
fight	**19**	打架
fly	**20**	飛
jump/leap	**21**	跳躍
kick	**22**	踢
kneel	**23**	跪
laugh	**24**	笑
lick	**25**	舐

listen **1** 聽	sing **14** 唱
open **2** 打開	sit **15** 坐
lie **3** 臥	smile **16** 微笑
paint **4** （用顏料）繪畫	stand **17** 站立
pull **5** 拉	stir **18** 攪拌
push **6** 推	sweep **19** 掃除
read **7** 閱讀	swim **20** 游泳
ride **8** 騎	tear **21** 撕開
run **9** 跑	touch **22** 觸摸
sail **10** 航海，揚帆	tie **23** 捆縛
sew **11** 縫紉	walk **24** 步行
shoot **12** 射	wash **25** 洗
shut **13** 關閉	

wave **1** 揮手，揮舞	pass/overtake **13** 超越
write **2** 寫字	frown **14** 皺眉
wind **3** 上弦	put **15** 放
bend **4** 使彎曲	spin **16** 旋轉
hit/beat **5** 打，擊	clap **17** 拍手
hug **6** 擁抱	iron **18** 熨衣服
kiss **7** 吻	sleep **19** 睡覺
pick **8** 採摘	hold **20** 拿着，握
throw **9** 拋	type **21** 打字
turn **10** 轉動	boil **22** 沸騰
give **11** 給	chop **23** 砍
comb **12** 梳	

carton	**1**	硬紙盒	crate **11**	板條箱
urn	**2**	茶水壺	trunk **12**	大衣箱，槓箱
briefcase	**3**	公事包	sack **13**	大袋，麻包袋
barrel	**4**	桶	cage **14**	籠
(hand)bag	**5**	（手）袋	carrier-bag **15**	手提袋
purse	**6**	錢包	wallet **16**	皮夾子
paper-bag	**7**	紙袋	(suit)case **17**	衣箱
dustbin	**8**	廢紙箱，垃圾桶	holdall **18**	手提袋
thermos/vacuum-flask	**9**	熱水瓶	box **19**	盒
			safe **20**	保險箱
(shopping) basket	**10**	（購物）籃子	(water-)tank **21**	（水）箱

Lines A. 綫條
spiral	**1**	螺旋綫
straight line	**2**	直綫
curve	**3**	曲綫
perpendicular line	**4**	垂直綫
parallel lines	**5**	平行綫
zig-zag	**6**	之字形綫
wavy line	**7**	波浪綫

Triangles B. 三角形
apex	**8**	頂點
base	**9**	底邊
obtuse angle	**10**	鈍角
acute angle	**11**	銳角
hypotenuse	**12**	斜邊

Square C. 正方形
side	**13**	邊
right angle	**14**	直角

Rectangle/Oblong D. 長方形
diagonal	**15**	對角綫

Circle E. 圓形
arc	**16**	弧
radius	**17**	半徑
circumference	**18**	圓周
diameter	**19**	直徑
centre	**20**	圓心
sector	**21**	扇形面

Oval/Ellipse F. 橢圓形

Solid Figures G. 立體形
pyramid	**22**	角錐體
cone	**23**	圓錐體
cube	**24**	立方體
cylinder	**25**	圓柱體

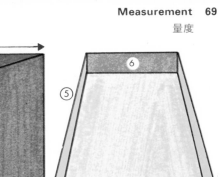

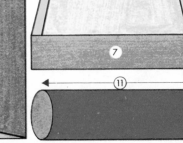

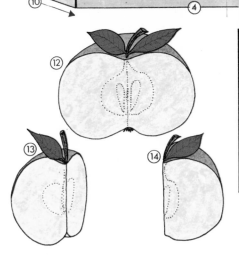

On the blackboard:

$$2 + 1 = 3 \qquad 2\%$$
$$2 \times 1 = 2 \qquad 2.5$$
$$2 - 1 = 1 \qquad 2\frac{1}{2}$$
$$2 \div 1 = 2$$

top	**1**	頂
bottom	**2**	底
corner	**3**	角
edge	**4**	邊緣
side	**5**	邊
back	**6**	反面，後面
front	**7**	前面
width	**8**	闊度
height	**9**	高度
depth	**10**	深度
length	**11**	長度

a half	**12**	一半，二分一
a third	**13**	三分一
a quarter	**14**	四分一
plus	**15**	加
multiplied by	**16**	乘
minus	**17**	減
divided by	**18**	除
equals	**19**	等於
per cent	**20**	百分比
decimal point	**21**	小數點
fraction	**22**	分數

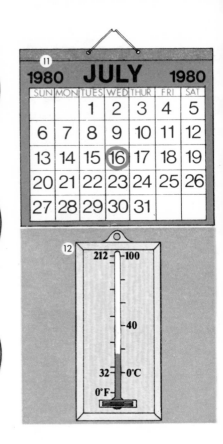

The Time A.	時間
minute hand 1	分針
hour hand 2	時針
second hand 3	秒針
clock face 4	鐘面
9:00: nine o'clock 5	九時正
9:10: ten past nine/nine ten 6	九時十分
9:15: (a) quarter past nine/nine fifteen 7	九時一刻，九時十五分
9:30: half past nine/nine thirty 8	九時半，九時三十分
9:45: a quarter to ten/nine forty-five 9	九時三刻，九時四十五分
9:50: ten to ten/nine fifty 10	九時五十分

The Date B.	日期
calendar 11	日曆
Today's date is Wednesday the sixteenth of July, nineteen eighty: 16th July 1980 or 16/7/80.	今天的日期是一九八零年七月十六日星期三

The Temperature C.	溫度
thermometer 12	溫度計
The temperature is 18 degrees Centigrade (18°C) or 65 degrees Fahrenheit (65°F)	溫度是攝氏十八度或華氏六十五度

1 Alan and Ann are **husband** and **wife**.
2 Their **children** are Betty and Bob.
3 Their **daughter** is Betty and their **son** is Bob.
4 Alan is Bob's **father** and Ann is Bob's **mother**.
5 Betty is Bob's **sister** and Bob is Betty's **brother**.
6 Alan is Ben's **father-in-law** and Ann is his **mother-in-law**.
7 Ben is Alan and Ann's **son-in-law** and Brenda is their **daughter-in-law**.
8 Ben is Bob's **brother-in-law** and Brenda is Betty's **sister-in-law**.
9 Colin is Cliff and Carol's **cousin**.
10 Betty is Colin's **aunt** and Ben is his **uncle**.
11 Colin is Betty's **nephew** and Carol is Bob's **niece**.
12 Cliff is Ann and Alan's **grandson** and Carol is their **granddaughter**.

1 亞倫和安是**夫婦**。
2 比提和鮑勃是他們的**兒女**。
3 比提是他們的**女兒**，鮑勃是他們的**兒子**。
4 亞倫是鮑勃的**父親**，安是鮑勃的**母親**。
5 比提是鮑勃的**姊妹**，鮑勃是比提的**兄弟**。
6 亞倫是班的**岳父**，安是他的**岳母**。
7 班是亞倫和安的**女婿**，布倫達是他們的**媳婦**。
8 班是鮑勃的**內兄**，布倫達是比提的**嫂子**。
9 科林是奇里夫和卡羅爾的**表親**。
10 比提是科林的**姑姑**，班是科林的**姑丈**。
11 科林是比提的**侄兒**，卡羅爾是鮑勃的**外甥女**。
12 奇里夫是安和亞倫的**男孫**，卡羅爾是他們的**女孫**。

bunch (of flowers)	**1**	一束（花）	
bundle (of sticks)	**2**	一捆（棍子）	heap (of stones) **9** 一堆（石頭）
crowd (of people)	**3**	一羣（人）	herd (of cows) **10** 一羣（牛）
fleet (of ships)	**4**	一隊（船）	party (of tourists) **11** 一羣（遊客）
flight (of stairs)	**5**	一段（樓梯）	pile (of blankets) **12** 一叠（毛氈）
flock (of sheep or birds)	**6**	一羣（羊或鳥）	plate (of sandwiches) **13** 一碟（三文治）
			row (of houses) **14** 一排（房屋）
gang (of workmen)	**7**	一組（工人）	team (of players) **15** 一隊（運動員）
string (of beads)	**8**	一串（珠子）	swarm (of bees) **16** 一窩（蜂）

ball (of string, wool)	**1**	一團（繩子，毛綫）	
bar (of chocolate)	**2**	一大塊（巧格力）	
tablet/bar (of soap)	**3**	一塊（肥皂）	
joint (of meat)	**4**	一大塊（肉）	
line (of washing)	**5**	一繩（洗淨的衣物）	
loaf (of bread)	**6**	一隻，一條（麵飽）	
lump (of sugar)	**7**	一塊，一粒（糖）	
slice/piece (of cake)	**8**	一件，一塊（糕餅）	

reel (of cotton)	**9**	一卷（綫）
box (of matches)/	**10**	一盒（火柴）
carton (of cigarettes)		一包（香煙）
packet (of tea)	**11**	一盒，一包（茶葉）
roll (of paper)	**12**	一卷（紙）
tube (of toothpaste)	**13**	一管（牙膏）
bowl (of soup)	**14**	一碗（湯）

big/large (a)	**1**	大的	fast (a)	**9**	快的
little/small (b)		小的	slow (b)		慢的
blunt (a)	**2**	鈍的	fat (a)	**10**	肥的
sharp (b)		銳利的	thin (b)		瘦的
clean (a)	**3**	清潔的	happy (a)	**11**	快樂的
dirty (b)		骯髒的	sad (b)		憂愁的
closed/shut (a)	**4**	關閉的	easy (a)	**12**	容易的
open (b)		開着的	difficult/hard (b)		困難的
crooked (a)	**5**	扭曲的	soft (a)	**13**	柔軟的
straight (b)		直的	hard (b)		堅硬的
shallow (a)	**6**	淺的	high (a)	**14**	高的
deep (b)		深的	low (b)		矮的
wet (a)	**7**	濕的	hot (a)	**15**	熱的
dry (b)		乾的	cold (b)		冷的
empty (a)	**8**	空的	long (a)	**16**	長的
full (b)		滿的	short (b)		短的

narrow (a)	**1**	窄的		pretty/beautiful (a)	**9**	美麗的
wide (b)		闊的		ugly (b)		醜陋的
young (a)	**2**	少的		first (a)	**10**	最先的
old (b)		老的		last (b)		最後的
new (a)	**3**	新的		light (a)	**11**	光明的
old (b)		舊的		dark (b)		黑暗的
calm (a)	**4**	平靜的		light (a)	**12**	輕的
rough (b)		洶湧的		heavy (b)		重的
rough (a)	**5**	粗糙的		loud (a)	**13**	響亮的
smooth (b)		平滑的		soft (b)		輕聲的
strong (a)	**6**	強壯的		solid (a)	**14**	實心的
weak (b)		虛弱的		hollow (b)		中空的
tidy (a)	**7**	整齊的		thick (a)	**15**	粗大的
untidy (b)		不整齊的、凌亂的		thin (b)		纖細的
good (a)	**8**	好的		loose (a)	**16**	鬆的
bad (b)		壞的		tight (b)		緊的

outside the room	**1**	在房子外	**out of** the drawer	**11**	在抽屜外
through the door	**2**	穿過門	**on** the table	**12**	在桌上
below the picture	**3**	在圖畫下	**on to/onto** the table	**13**	放在桌上
down the wall	**4**	在牆下方	**beside/next to** the table	**14**	在桌旁
up the wall	**5**	在牆上方	**by/near** the chair	**15**	在椅子旁
round the neck	**6**	在頸的週圍	**behind** the chair	**16**	在椅子後
in front of the chair	**7**	在梯子前	**under/underneath** the table	**17**	在桌下
against the wall	**8**	靠着牆			
into the drawer	**9**	進抽屜裏			
in/inside the drawer	**10**	在抽屜裏			

above the trees	1	在樹叢上方	**at** the corner	8	在拐角那裏
beyond the bridge	2	橋的那邊	**along** the road	9	沿着公路
from the sea	3	由海那邊來	**towards** the bridge	10	向着橋
to the sea	4	向海那邊去	**away from** the	11	遠離橋
among the trees	5	在樹叢間	bridge		
off the road	6	離開公路	**between** the cars	12	在兩車之間
across/over the road	7	橫過公路			

A. **This** boy is Paul. **He** is holding **his** football. **It** is **his**. He says, "I am Paul. **This** is **my** football. It is **mine**. **Its** colours are black and white."

B. This girl is Mary. **She** is riding **her** bicycle. It is **hers**. She says, "My father gave it to **me**."

C. Paul and Mary have a dog. He is **theirs**. **They** are feeding **their** dog. Bob is watching **them**. Mary says to Bob, "This is **our** dog. He is **ours**. He belongs to **us**. **We** are feeding **him**." Bob says, "This is water for **your** dog."

D. Paul says to Bob, "**Who** is **that** girl **there**?" Bob says, "**That** is Julie. She is coming **here**."

E. Bob says to Julie, "**What** are **those** things **you** are carrying?" Julie says, "**These** are oranges." Paul says, "**Whose** oranges are they?" Julie says, "They are for **you** and Bob. They are **yours**." Bob says, "**Which one** is mine?" Julie says, "This one here. But **where** is Mary? **This** one is for **her**."

下列為說明性的譯文。目的在表示英文代名詞及所有格在英文句子內的用法,請注意中英文黑體字的對應關係。

A. 這個男孩是保羅。他正拿着他的足球。它是他的。他說:「我是保羅。這是我的足球。它是我的。它的顏色是黑和白的。」

B. 這個女孩是瑪利。她正在騎着她的腳踏車。它是她的。她說:「我父親送它給我的。」

C. 保羅和瑪利有一頭狗。他是他們的。他們正在餵他們的狗。鮑勃正在看着他們。瑪利對鮑勃說:「這是我們的狗。他是我們的。他是屬於我們的。我們正在餵他。」鮑勃說:「這些水給你們的狗。」

D. 保羅對鮑勃說:「那邊那個女孩是誰?」鮑勃說:「那是茱莉。她正向這邊走來。」

E. 鮑勃對茱莉說:「你拿着的是些甚麼東西?」茱莉說:「這些是橘子。」保羅說:「它們是誰的?」茱莉說:「它們是給你和鮑勃的。它們是你們的。」鮑勃說:「那一個是我的?」茱莉說:「這個。瑪利在那裏? 這個給她。」

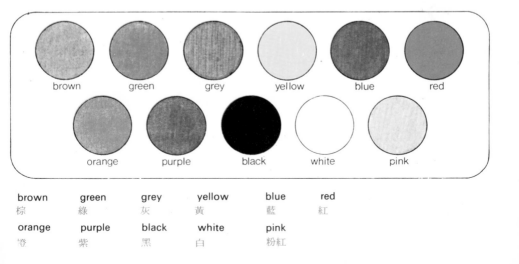

brown	green	grey	yellow	blue	red
棕	綠	灰	黃	藍	紅

orange	purple	black	white	pink
橙	紫	黑	白	粉紅

Numerals 數目

nought, zero \ nothing	**0** 零		forty **40** 四十
one	**1** 一		fifty **50** 五十
two	**2** 二		sixty **60** 六十
three	**3** 三		seventy **70** 七十
four	**4** 四		eighty **80** 八十
five	**5** 五		ninety **90** 九十
six	**6** 六		a/one hundred **100** 一百
seven	**7** 七		five hundred **500** 五百
eight	**8** 八		six hundred and **621** 六百二十一
nine	**9** 九		twenty-one
ten	**10** 十		a/one thousand **1,000** 一千
eleven	**11** 十一		a million **1,000,000** 一百萬
twelve	**12** 十二		first **1st** 第一
thirteen	**13** 十三		second **2nd** 第二
fourteen	**14** 十四		third **3rd** 第三
fifteen	**15** 十五		fourth **4th** 第四
sixteen	**16** 十六		fifth **5th** 第五
seventeen	**17** 十七		sixth **6th** 第六
eighteen	**18** 十八		seventh **7th** 第七
nineteen	**19** 十九		eighth **8th** 第八
twenty	**20** 二十		ninth **9th** 第九
twenty-one	**21** 二十一		tenth **10th** 第十
thirty	**30** 三十		twentieth **20th** 第二十

Weight
1,000 grams (gm) = 1 kilogram (kg)

重量
1,000克＝1千克（公斤）

Length
10 millimetres (mm) = 1 centimetre (cm)
100 centimetres = 1 metre (m)
1,000 metres = 1 kilometre (km)

長度
10毫米＝1厘米
100厘米＝1米
1,000米＝1千米（公里）

Liquids
1,000 millilitres (ml) = 1 litre (l)

容量
1,000毫升＝1升

Time
60 seconds = 1 minute (min)
60 minutes = 1 hour (hr)
24 hours = 1 day
7 days = 1 week (wk)
365 days = 1 year (yr)
12 months = 1 year
100 years = 1 century (c)

時間
60秒 ＝1分
60分 ＝1小時
24小時＝1天
7天 ＝1星期
365天 ＝1年
12月 ＝1年
100年 ＝1世紀

Days of the Week
星期
Monday, Tuesday, Wednesday, Thursday, Friday, Saturday, Sunday.
星期一， 星期二， 星期三， 星期四， 星期五, 星期六, 星期日

Months of the Year
月份
January, February, March, April, May, June, July, August, September,
October, November, December.
一月, 二月, 三月, 四月, 五月, 六月, 七月, 八月, 九月, 十月, 十一月, 十二月

元音及雙元音

i	as in *sea*	/si/	ʊ	as in *book*	/bʊk/	ɪə	as in *five*	/faɪv/
ɪ	as in *sit*	/sɪt/	u	as in *root*	/rut/	aʊ	as in *mouse*	/maʊs/
e	as in *ten*	/ten/	ʌ	as in *cup*	/kʌp/	ɔɪ	as in *toy*	/tɔɪ/
æ	as in *hut*	/hæt/	ɜ	as in *fur*	/fɜ(r)/	ɪə	as in *near*	/nɪə(r)/
ɑ	as in *farm*	/fɑm/	ə	as in *away*	/ə`weɪ/	eə	as in *hair*	/heə(r)/
o	as in *pot*	/pɒt/	eɪ	as in *page*	/peɪdʒ/	ʊə	as in *pure*	/pjʊə(r)/
ɔ	as in *ball*	/bɔl/	əʊ	as in *hole*	/həʊl/			

輔音

p	as in *pen*	/pen/	f	as in *five*	/faɪv/	h	as in *hair*	/heə(r)/
b	as in *ball*	/bɔl/	v	as in *van*	/væn/	m	as in *mouse*	/maʊs/
t	as in *toy*	/tɔɪ/	θ	as in *thin*	/θɪn/	n	as in *neck*	/nek/
d	as in *dog*	/dɒg/	ð	as in *there*	/ðeə(r)/	ŋ	as in *wing*	/wɪŋ/
k	as in *cat*	/kæt/	s	as in *sea*	/si/	l	as in *ball*	/bɔl/
g	as in *goat*	/gəʊt/	z	as in *zip*	/zɪp/	r	as in *root*	/rut/
tʃ	as in *chin*	/tʃɪn/	ʃ	as in *she*	/ʃi/	j	as in *year*	/jɪə(r)/
dʒ	as in *jaw*	/dʒɔ/	ʒ	as in *measure*	/`meʒə(r)/	w	as in *wing*	/wɪŋ/

Index

laundry-basket /'lɔːndrɪ bɑːskɪt/ 33/26
lavatory /'lævətrɪ/ 33/7
law /lɔː/ 16
'law court 16/C
lawn /lɔːn/ 27/19
lawyer /'lɔːjə(r)/ 16/23
leaf /liːf/ 63/15
leap /liːp/ 64/21
leaves /liːvz/ 27/15
ledge /ledʒ/ 26/11
left /left/ 47/15, 17, 20, 21
leg /leg/ 8/32
‡leisure /'leʒə(r)/ 50
lemon /'lemən/ 61/14
length /leŋθ/ 69/11; 80/B
lens /lenz/ 19/10; 52/26
leopard /'lepəd/ 57/18
letter /'letə(r)/ 22/7, 10
'letter-basket 21/12
'letter-box 14/1; 22/4; 28/5
lettuce /'letɪs/ 62/12
librarian /laɪˈbreərɪən/ 50/22
library /'laɪbrərɪ/ 50
lick /lɪk/ 64/25
lid /lɪd/ 29/35
lie /laɪ/ 65/3
light /laɪt/ 14/7; 17/18; 28/22; 38/4, 5, 29;
  40/30; 44/17; 75/11, 12
'light-bulb 31/13
‡lightning /'laɪtnɪŋ/ 27/1
'light-switch 28/13
line /laɪn/ 5/14, 15; 27/28; 47/8, 12, 13;
  48/20, 26; 68/A; 73/5
liner /'laɪnə(r)/ 43/20
linesman /'laɪnzmən/ 47/2
'line-up 47/C
lion /'laɪən/ 57/16
lip /lɪp/ 9/13
lipstick 12/19
liquid /'lɪkwɪd/ 30/28; 80/C
listen /'lɪsn/ 65/1
litre /'liːtə(r)/ 80
litter-bin/-basket· /'lɪtə(r)/ 15/30
little /'lɪtl/ 74/1
liver /'lɪvə(r)/ 9/25
living-room /'lɪvɪŋ rʊm/ 29
lizard /'lɪzəd/ 59/9
llama /'lɑːmə/ 56/5
loaf /ləʊf/ 73/6
lobster /'lɒbstə(r)/ 58/12
lock /lɒk/ 28/7
locust /'ləʊkəst/ 59/10
log /lɒg/ 63/18
long /lɒŋ/ 74/16
longitude /'lɒndʒɪtjuːd/ 5/14
loo /luː/ 33/7
loose /luːs/ 75/16
lorry /'lɒrɪ/ 14/15; 39/14
loud /laʊd/ 75/13
loudspeaker /ˌlaʊdˈspiːkə(r)/ 49/28
low /ləʊ/ 74/14
‡luggage /'lʌgɪdʒ/ 44/4
'luggage-rack 41/9
lump /lʌmp/ 73/7
lung /lʌŋ/ 9/24
lychee /ˌlaɪˈtʃiː/ 61/26

mac /mæk/ 11/12
machine /məˈʃiːn/ 31/4; 53/1
maˈchine-gun 45/15
mackintosh /'mækɪntɒʃ/ 11/12
magnet /'mægnɪt/ 19/19
magnifying-glass /'mægnɪfaɪɪŋ glɑːs/ 16/10
mailbag /'meɪlbæg/ 22/6
‡maize /meɪz/ 63/1
mallet /'mælɪt/ 25/1
man /mæn/ 10–11
mane /meɪn/ 57/17
mango /'mæŋgəʊ/ 61/15
mantelpiece /'mæntlpiːs/ 29/5
mantis /'mæntɪs/ 59/15
map /mæp/ 5/B; 18/21
March /mɑːtʃ/ 80
market /'mɑːkɪt/ 14/3
marrow /'mærəʊ/ 62/7
‡mascara /mæˈskɑːrə/ 12/14
mask /mɑːsk/ 35/15; 48/2
mast /mɑːst/ 43/3
mat /mæt/ 26/18; 28/10; 29/25; 33/23
match /mætʃ/ 51/16
'matchbox 51/5
material /məˈtɪərɪəl/ 53/13
mattock /'mætək/ 23/19

mattress /'mætrɪs/ 32/8
May /meɪ/ 80
me /miː/ 79
meadow /'medəʊ/ 34/11
measure /'meʒə(r)/ 53/25; 80
measurement /'meʒəmənt/ 69
‡meat /miːt/ 20/13
mechanic /mɪˈkænɪk/ 54/5
medical /'medɪkl/ 17
medicine /'medsɪn/ 17/30
Mediterranean /ˌmedɪtəˈreɪnɪən/ 6/22
Mekong /miːˈkɒŋ/ 7/53
menu /'menjuː/ 51/23
meter /'miːtə(r)/ 19/4
metre /'miːtə(r)/ 80
Mexico (Gulf of) /'meksɪkəʊ/ 6/17
microphone /'maɪkrəfəʊn/ 49/25
microscope /'maɪkrəskəʊp/ 19/9
midfield /'mɪdfiːld/ 47/17, 18, 19
mike /maɪk/ 49/25
milk /mɪlk/ 20/10
'milk-jug 29/37
millilitre /'mɪlɪliːtə(r)/ 80
millimetre /'mɪlɪmiːtə(r)/ 80
million /'mɪljən/ 80
mine /maɪn/ 79
miner /'maɪnə(r)/ 54/7
minus /'maɪnəs/ 69/17
minute /'mɪnɪt/ 70/1; 80
mirror /'mɪrə(r)/ 32/12; 38/1; 40/3
missile /'mɪsaɪl/ 45/4
Mississippi /ˌmɪsɪˈsɪpɪ/ 7/45
mixer /'mɪksə(r)/ 23/21
Monday /'mʌndeɪ/ 80
monkey /'mʌŋkɪ/ 57/13
month /mʌnθ/ 80
Moon /muːn/ 4/6
mop /mɒp/ 31/5
mortar /'mɔːtə(r)/ 19/21
mosquito /məˈskiːtəʊ/ 59/20
moth /mɒθ/ 59/26
mother /'mʌðə(r)/ 71/4
mother-in-law /'mʌðər ɪn lɔː/ 71/6
motor /'məʊtə(r)/ 43/13
'motorbike/cycle 14/17; 39/20
'motor-boat 35/34; 43/12
'motor-car 38
'motor-launch 43/12
'motorway 39/1
mountain /'maʊntɪn/ 34/2
mountain 'range 7
mouse /maʊs/ 56/18
moustache /məˈstɑːʃ/ 9/10
mouth /maʊθ/ 9/4
'mouthpiece 49/23
mudguard /'mʌdgɑːd/ 40/10
mug /mʌg/ 51/3
multiply by /'mʌltɪplaɪ/ 69/16
muscle /'mʌsl/ 9/31
mushroom /'mʌʃrʊm/ 62/14
‡music /'mjuːzɪk/ 49
musician /mjuːˈzɪʃn/ 49/3
‡mustard /'mʌstəd/ 51/28
my /maɪ/ 79

nail /neɪl/ 8/31; 25/11
'nail-brush 33/18
'nail-file 12/12
‡'nail-polish 12/15
‡'nail-varnish 12/15
napkin /'næpkɪn/ 51/31
nappy /'næpɪ/ 32/36
narrow /'nærəʊ/ 75/1
national /'næʃənl/ 45
navigator /'nævɪgeɪtə(r)/ 45/26
Navy /'neɪvɪ/ 45/B
near /nɪə(r)/ 76/15
neck /nek/ 8/11
necklace /'neklɪs/ 12/11
needle /'niːdl/ 5/16; 19/6; 53/6, 18; 63/22
negative /'negətɪv/ 52/23
nephew /'nevjuː/ 71/11
nest /nest/ 60/29
net /net/ 46/20; 48/24
new /njuː/ 4/11; 75/3
,new 'moon 4/11
next /nekst/ 76/14
niece /niːs/ 71/11
Niger /'naɪdʒə(r)/ 7/49
nightdress /'naɪtdres/ 12/6
'nightgown 12/6
Nile /naɪl/ 7/48
nine /naɪn/ 80

nineteen /naɪnˈtiːn/ 80
ninety /'naɪntɪ/ 80
ninth /naɪnθ/ 80
north /nɔːθ/ 5/C
northeast /ˌnɔːθˈiːst/ 5/C
,North 'Pole 5/1
,North 'Sea 6/20
northwest /ˌnɔːθˈwest/ 5/C
nose /nəʊz/ 9/2
nosecone /'nəʊzkəʊn/ 4/15
note /nəʊt/ 20/24
'notebook 21/23
'notepad 21/23
nothing /'nʌθɪŋ/ 80
noun /naʊn/ 72
nought /nɔːt/ 80
November /nəʊˈvembə(r)/ 80
nozzle /'nɒzl/ 17/4
number /'nʌmbə(r)/ 41/21; 80
'number-plate 38/28
nurse /nɜːs/ 17/14, 25; 55/10
nut /nʌt/ 25/13; 61/11, 27

oak /əʊk/ 63/10
oar /ɔː(r)/ 43/7
object /'ɒbdʒɪkt/ 31
oblong /'ɒblɒŋ/ 68/D
obtuse /əbˈtjuːs/ 68/10
occupation /ˌɒkjʊˈpeɪʃn/ 54–55
ocean /'əʊʃn/ 6/B
o'clock /əˈklɒk/ 70/5
October /ɒkˈtəʊbə(r)/ 80
octopus /'ɒktəpəs/ 58/23
off /ɒf/ 77/6
office /'ɒfɪs/ 21; 41/14
'office-block 15/20
oil-derrick /'ɔɪl derɪk/ 37/10
oil-rig /'ɔɪl rɪg/ 37/11
oil-tanker /'ɔɪl tæŋkə(r)/ 43/18
Okhotsk (Sea of) /əʊˈkɒtsk/ 7/34
old /əʊld/ 4/14; 75/2, 3
olive /'ɒlɪv/ 63/3
on /ɒn/ 76/12
one /wʌn/ 79–80
onion /'ʌnjən/ 62/13
onto /'ɒntʊ/ 76/13 ·
open /'əʊpən/ 65/2; 74/4
opener /'əʊpnə(r)/ 51/7
operator /'ɒpəreɪtə(r)/ 21/16
optician /ɒpˈtɪʃn/ 55/14
orange /'ɒrɪndʒ/ 61/16; 79
orbit /'ɔːbɪt/ 4/9
orchard /'ɔːtʃəd/ 36/12
orchestra /'ɔːkɪstrə/ 49/A; 50/12
orchid /'ɔːkɪd/ 62/21
ostrich /'ɒstrɪtʃ/ 60/1
our /'aʊə(r)/ 79
ours /'aʊəz/ 79
out /aʊt/ 76/11
outboard motor /ˌaʊtbɔːd ˈməʊtə(r)/ 43/13
outside /ˌaʊtˈsaɪd/ 47/20, 24; 76/1
,outside-'lane 39/5
oval /'əʊvl/ 68/F
oven /'ʌvn/* 30/2
over /'əʊvə(r)/ 77/7
overtake /ˌəʊvəˈteɪk/ 66/13
owl /aʊl/ 60/7
oyster /'ɔɪstə(r)/ 58/16

Pacific /pəˈsɪfɪk/ 6/9, 10
pack /pæk/ 52/10
packet /'pækɪt/ 73/11
pad /pæd/ 21/4, 23; 48/12
paddle /'pædl/ 43/9
page /peɪdʒ/ 52/19
paint /peɪnt/ 18/27; 65/4
'paintbrush 18/25
palette /'pælət/ 18/26
palm /pɑːm/ 8/28; 63/19
pan /pæn/ 19/2; 30/11, 12
pane /peɪn/ 26/10
panel /'pænl/ 45/28
pannier /'pænɪə(r)/ 40/34
†pants /pænts/ 10/2; 12/3
papaya /pəˈpaɪə/ 61/25
paper /'peɪpə(r)/ 21/10, 20; 22/12; 24/3; 33/9
,paper-'bag 67/7
'paper-clip 21/9
parachute /'pærəʃuːt/ 45/25
parallel /'pærəlel/ 68/5
parcel /'pɑːsl/ 22/20
park /pɑːk/ 14/12, 32
parking-meter /'pɑːkɪŋ miːtə(r)/ 15/25

scarecrow /'skeəkrəʊ/ 36/13
scarf /skɑːf/ 11/19; 13/13
‡scent /sent/ 12/16
school /skuːl/ 18
'schoolbag 18/9
'schoolgirl 18/8
science /'saɪəns/ 19
†scissors /'sɪzəz/ 53/26
scooter /'skuːtə(r)/ 40/29
scorpion /'skɔːpɪən/ 58/27
scourer /'skaʊrə(r)/ 30/26
‡scouring powder /'skaʊrɪŋ paʊdə(r)/ 31/9
screen /skriːn/ 29/18; 50/18; 52/27
screw /skruː/ 25/9
screwdriver /'skruːdraɪvə(r)/ 24/7
scrubbing-brush /'skrʌbɪŋ brʌʃ/ 31/10
sea /siː/ 6–7/C; 35/31
'sea-front 35/9
'seagull 60/21
seal /siːl/ 22/18; 57/9
‡sealing-wax /'siːlɪŋ wæks/ 22/19
seam /siːm/ 53/3
‡seaside 35/B
seat /siːt/ 38/23; 40/31; 41/8; 50/20
'seat-belt 38/24
,sea-'wall 35/10
‡seaweed /'siːwiːd/ 35/37
second /'sekənd/ 70/3; 80
secretary /'sekrətrɪ/ 21/22
sector /'sektə(r)/ 68/21
seed /siːd/ 62/28
segment /'segmənt/ 61/17
September /sep'tembə(r)/ 80
server /'sɜːvə(r)/ 48/25
service /'sɜːvɪs/ 17; 48/26
'service-station 39/7
serviette /,sɜːvɪ'et/ 51/31
set /set/ 50/4
'set-square 18/16
settee /se'tiː/ 29/21
seven /'sevn/ 80
seventeen /,sevn'tiːn/ 80
seventh /'sevnθ/ 80
seventy /'sevntɪ/ 80
sew /səʊ/ 65/11
sewing /'səʊɪŋ/ 53
'sewing-machine 53/1
shallow /'ʃæləʊ/ 74/6
shape /ʃeɪp/ 68
shark /ʃɑːk/ 58/1
sharp /ʃɑːp/ 74/2
shaving-brush /'ʃeɪvɪŋ brʌʃ/ 33/14
shawl /ʃɔːl/ 12/5
she /ʃiː/ 79
†shears /ʃɪəz/ 24/11
shed /ʃed/ 26/20; 27/26
‡†sheep /ʃiːp/ 36/29
'sheepdog 36/28
sheet /ʃiːt/ 21/10; 32/5; 49/12
shelf /ʃelf/ 20/15; 30/16
shell /ʃel/ 35/27; 45/7; 58/14; 59/5
shepherd /'ʃepəd/ 36/26
ship /ʃɪp/ 42/7
shirt /ʃɜːt/ 11/1
shoe /ʃuː/ 10/9; 11/8; 13/12
shoelace /'ʃuːleɪs/ 11/9
shoot /ʃuːt/ 65/12
shop /ʃɒp/ 15/22
'shop-assistant 20/8
'shopping basket 67/10
,shop-'window 15/23; 20/1
short /ʃɔːt/ 74/16
†shorts /ʃɔːts/ 10/12
shoulder /'ʃəʊldə(r)/ 8/13
'shoulder-blade 8/3
shovel /'ʃʌvl/ 23/13
shower /'ʃaʊə(r)/ 33/4
shrub /ʃrʌb/ 27/22
shut /ʃʌt/ 65/13; 74/4
shutter /'ʃʌtə(r)/ 26/12
side /saɪd/ 68/13; 69/5
siding /'saɪdɪŋ/ 41/30
sieve /sɪv/ 30/30
signal /'sɪgnl/ 41/27
'signal-box 41/23
'signalman 41/22
signpost /'saɪnpəʊst/ 14/8
sill /sɪl/ 26/11
sing /sɪŋ/ 65/14
singer /'sɪŋə(r)/ 49/24
sink /sɪŋk/ 30/7
sister /'sɪstə(r)/ 71/5
sister-in-law /'sɪstər ɪn lɔː/ 71/8

sit /sɪt/ 65/15
site /saɪt/ 23
sitting-room /'sɪtɪŋ rʊm/ 29
six /sɪks/ 80
sixteen /,sɪks'tiːn/ 80
sixth /sɪksθ/ 80
sixty /'sɪkstɪ/ 80
skate /skeɪt/ 47/31
skater /'skeɪtə(r)/ 47/30
skeleton /'skelɪtn/ 8/A
ski /skiː/ 47/26
skier /'skiːə(r)/ 47/25
‡skin /skɪn/ 61/3
skip /skɪp/ 23/24
'ski-pole 47/27
skirt /skɜːt/ 13/2
'ski-stick 47/27
skull /skʌl/ 8/1
sky /skaɪ/ 27/10
sleep /sliːp/ 66/19
sleeper /'sliːpə(r)/ 41/25
sleeping-bag /'sliːpɪŋ bæg/ 35/3
'sleeping suit 32/27
sleeve /sliːv/ 11/7
slice /slaɪs/ 73/8
slide /slaɪd/ 19/11; 49/21; 52/30
'slide-projector 52/29
'slide-rule 18/20
sling /slɪŋ/ 17/23
slip /slɪp/ 12/2; 32/4
slipper /'slɪpə(r)/ 10/5; 12/7
slow /sləʊ/ 74/9
slug /slʌg/ 58/19
small /smɔːl/ 74/1
smile /smaɪl/ 65/16
‡smoke /sməʊk/ 17/12
smooth /smuːð/ 75/5
snail /sneɪl/ 58/13
snake /sneɪk/ 59/6
snapshot /'snæpʃɒt/ 52/22
snorkel /'snɔːkl/ 35/16
snout /snaʊt/ 56/4; 58/8
‡snow /snəʊ/ 27/5
'snowball 27/6
'snowman 27/7
‡soap /səʊp/ 33/25
‡soap powder /'səʊp paʊdə(r)/ 31/18
‡soccer /'sɒkə(r)/ 47/A
sock /sɒk/ 10/14; 13/3
socket /'sɒkɪt/ 31/16
sofa /'səʊfə/ 29/21
soft /sɒft/ 51/13; 74/13
soldier /'səʊldʒə(r)/ 45/1; 55/12
sole /səʊl/ 9/40; 11/10
solid /'sɒlɪd/ 68/G; 75/14
son /sʌn/ 71/3
son-in-law /'sʌn ɪn lɔː/ 71/7
south /saʊθ/ 5/C
South ,China 'Sea 7/31
southeast /,saʊθ'iːst/ 5/C
Southern /'sʌðən/ 6/14
,South 'Pole 5/7
southwest /,saʊθ'west/ 5/C
‡space /speɪs/ 4
'space-capsule 4/19
'spacesuit 4/21
‡'space-travel 4/C
spade /speɪd/ 24/9; 35/25; 52/14
spanner /'spænə(r)/ 24/13
sparking-plug /'spɑːkɪŋ plʌg/ 38/35
sparrow /'spærəʊ/ 60/28
speedometer /spɪ'dɒmɪtə(r)/ 38/16
spider /'spaɪdə(r)/ 58/25
spin /spɪn/ 66/16
spine /spaɪn/ 8/6; 52/18
spiral /'spaɪərəl/ 68/1
spoke /spəʊk/ 40/12
sponge /spʌndʒ/ 33/24
spoon /spuːn/ 17/31; 29/27
sport /spɔːt/ 46–48
sportscar /'spɔːtskɑː(r)/ 39/18
spot /spɒt/ 47/11
'spotlight 50/7
spout /spaʊt/ 29/34
square /skweə(r)/ 68/C
squirrel /'skwɪrəl/ 56/19
stadium /'steɪdɪəm/ 47/B
stage /steɪdʒ/ 50/1
stair /steə(r)/ 28/16
'staircase 28/17
stalk /stɔːk/ 61/2; 62/2
stall /stɔːl/ 14/3
stalls /stɔːlz/ 50/11

stamp /stæmp/ 22/9
stand /stænd/ 47/5; 52/28; 65/17
staple /'steɪpl/ 21/8
stapler /'steɪplə(r)/ 21/7
star /stɑː(r)/ 4/5
starter /'stɑːtə(r)/ 40/36
station /'steɪʃn/ 41/13
steering-wheel /'stɪərɪŋ wiːl/ 38/17
stem /stem/ 62/23
stethoscope /'steθəskəʊp/ 17/22
stick /stɪk/ 46/18; 47/27
stir /stɜː(r)/ 65/18
stirrup /'stɪrəp/ 46/7
stitch /stɪtʃ/ 53/17
stomach /'stʌmək/ 8/17
stone /stəʊn/ 61/8, 20
stool /stuːl/ 19/8; 32/11; 49/18; 51/20
storage tank /'stɔːrɪdʒ tæŋk/ 37/14
storm-cloud /'stɔːm klaʊd/ 27/2
stove /stəʊv/ 30/1; 35/5
straight /streɪt/ 68/2; 74/5
strainer /'streɪnə(r)/ 30/30
straw /strɔː/ 51/12
strawberry /'strɔːbrɪ/ 61/21
stream /striːm/ 34/1
street /striːt/ 15/34
stretcher /'stretʃə(r)/ 17/32
striker /'straɪkə(r)/ 47/20–24
‡string /strɪŋ/ 22/21; 49/5; 72/8
strong /strɒŋ/ 75/6
stumps /stʌmps/ 48/9
submarine /,sʌbmə'riːn/ 45/19
sugar-bowl /'ʃʊgə bəʊl/ 29/39
‡sugar cane /'ʃʊgə keɪn/ 63/9
suit /suːt/ 11/6; 46/23
suitcase 67/17
sun /sʌn/ 4/8; 27/9
'sunbather 35/33
Sunday /'sʌndɪ/ 80
‡†'sunfish 58/16
'sunflower 62/27
'sunshade 35/12
supermarket /'suːpəmɑːkɪt/ 20
‡surf sɜːf/ 35/32
swallow /'swɒləʊ/ 60/22
swan /swɒn/ 60/16
swarm /swɔːm/ 72/16
sweater /'swetə(r)/ 13/5
sweep /swiːp/ 65/19
swim /swɪm/ 65/20
swimming /'swɪmɪŋ/
'swimming-costume 35/36
'swimming trunks 35/20
switch /swɪtʃ/ 28/23; 31/17
'switchboard 21/15
‡‡swordfish /'sɔːdfɪʃ/ 58/3
symbol /'sɪmbl/ 81

T-shirt /'tiː ʃɜːt/ 10/11
table /'teɪbl/ 29/19, 23; 32/9, 10; 46/21
'table-cloth 51/30
'table-mat 29/25
tablet /'tæblɪt/ 73/3
‡'table-tennis 46/E
tail, /teɪl/ 44/13; 56/23; 58/7
tank /tæŋk/ 37/14; 45/8; 67/21
tankard /'tæŋkəd/ 51/14
tanker /'tæŋkə(r)/ 39/19; 43/18
tap /tæp/ 33/2, 3
tape /teɪp/ 53/2
'tape-measure 53/25
Tasman Sea /,tæzmən 'siː/ 6/30
taxi /'tæksɪ/ 14/5
tea /tiː/ 63/8
teacher /'tiːtʃə(r)/ 18/1; 55/11
team /tiːm/ 72/15
'teapot 29/36
tear /teə(r)/ 65/21
teat /tiːt/ 32/34
'tea-towel 30/32
teddy-bear /'tedɪ beə(r)/ 32/29
telegram /'telɪgræm/ 22/16
telephone /'telɪfəʊn/ 21/2; 28/25
telephone-box 15/31
'telephone directory 28/29
television /'telɪvɪʒn/ 29/17, 18
temperature /'temprətʃə(r)/ 70/C
temple /'templ/ 9/7
ten /ten/ 80
tennis /'tenɪs/ 46/E; 48/D
'tennis-ball 48/28
'tennis-shoe 10/15
tent /tent/ 35/1

索引

This Reprint Authorized by Oxford University Press
for Sales in Taiwan only.

First printing............... August 1982

Published by

THE CRANE PUBLISHING CO., LTD.
TAIPEI, TAIWAN 106
THE REPUBLIC OF CHINA
Tel: 393-4497, 986-3127

台 灣 版

著作者：Wendy Harris
發行人：**戴 奕 煌**
發行所：**文鶴出版有限公司**
地　址：台北市和平東路1段107號之3二樓
電　話：**393－4497**
總經銷：**衆 文 圖 書 公 司**
印刷所：台北市重慶南路一段九號
電　話：**371－7328**
郵政劃撥：第104880號
印刷所：**今日彩色印刷股份有限公司**
電　話：**3072803・3073665**
行政院新聞局局版台業字第一四五二號

中華民國七十一年八月初版
書一冊　　特價**100**元
錄音帶二卷特價**280**元